"Strong voice. Right values
Warren Bennis
Distinguished Professor, U

"This book has broad app
follow the examples sugge
sight."
Charles Grassley
U. S. Senator, Iowa, Chairman, Senate Finance Committee

"The best of contemporary business planning combined with stubborn loyalty to mature Christian ethics makes a stirring success story."
Dr. David W. Preus, Bishop Emeritus, American Lutheran Church

"Irv Burling has, by personal example, demonstrated that a disciplined proactive mindset can be a powerful catalyst for organizational renewal—a mark of enlightened leadership."
Ed Oakley, coauthor of Enlightened Leadership

"While Burling never uses the term "ethics," this a book about business ethics and how ethics can be integrated with skillful and creative management in the interest of bottom line profits and engendering human flourishing for employees, policyholders, and the communities in which his corporation existed."
Donald G. Jones, Professor Emeritus of Applied Social Ethics,
Drew University, Madison, New Jersey

"This is an excellent book for every business management team and Board of Directors interested in building a sustainable future in the 21st century. The book, informal in style and well written, provides sound theoretical underpinnings as well as many practical examples of what to do and what to avoid."
Bill Rabel, PhD., FLMI, CLU, Sr VP Life Office Management Association, (Ret.)

"Irv Burling lives every word in this book. He is a living example of this quote by Gandhi that "You will find yourself by losing yourself in service to others." He is a lifelong learner. He brings a long life of heart and wisdom to this book.

If you are looking for someone or some concepts to trust in, then this book is for you."
L. A. Reding, National Coach, President, LA & Company

"Using Micah 6:8 and Ephesians 4:2 as bookends to a very fine work, Irv Burling models the qualities described in these two biblical texts and writes with a servant heart. With passion and through clear illustrations Irv provides a significant counter weight to the proliferation of greed and pride which so plague today's marketplace."
Leroy R. Rehrer, Senior Pastor, Holy Trinity Lutheran Church

In Irv's book, *Winning Without Greed,* we are taught the great lesson that to get, we must give, that to accumulate, we must scatter, that to make ourselves happy, we must make others happy, and that in order to become spiritually vigorous, we must seek the spiritual good of others.
Jim Mudd, Senior, Chief Spiritual Officer, The Mudd Group

"Irv is a leader of faith, insight, courage, humility, wisdom, and compassion who knows that his vision must be congruent with the soul of those he was called to serve. His use of the powerful message of Scripture has led him through a very successful organizational transformation. I am recommending this book to every leader who is facing the challenges of rapid and unpredictable change."
Wayne Weissenbuehler, ELCA Synod Bishop, Rocky MT. Synod, Retired

"My wife and I found it outstanding. It tells the story of a CEO who, with extraordinary transparency, subjected himself to rigorous evaluation, engaged in self-examination and brought his Christian values to bear on the difficult business decisions that confronted him. The outcome of this story proves that business leaders who take into consideration ethical concerns like the well-being of employees and the impact of company decisions on local communities and are willing to be vulnerable can achieve striking success."
Rev. Dr. Jerry Folk, Executive Director, Wisc. Council of Churches, Retired

"I'm inspired when a talented corporate leader teaches others about shoul-

.dens for the sake of the wider community. Irv Burlings ethical con-
.s out of a belief that connects private faith and public avocation. Here
.r employs astute business acumen, great leadership instincts and his
. for others in creative tension. No amount of money can buy the profound
.pect and gratitude of the lives he affected. Many of his leadership principles
apply to other arenas, including the church."
Peter Strommen, ELCA Synod Bishop

"Irv challenges the all too prevalent theory in corporate America that the
bottom line is not only everything—it's the only thing that counts. With caring
Bible-based courage Irv demonstrates a refreshing approach that considers the
interests of all the stakeholders in the corporation"
John Beem, Bishop, East Central Synod of Wisconsin, Retired

"Irv Burling has written a book not only for business and organizations but
also for every one who wishes to move from human doing to becoming a
human being. It shares a vision of a future with hope."
Rev. Dr. Charles Berdahl, Regional Representative ELCA Board of Pension

"This book is an insightful and rich resource for any CEO involved in transforming an organization and its culture to meet the competitive challenges of
the 21st century."
John Kapanke, President/CEO, Board of Pensions
Evangelical Lutheran Church in America

"Selfless leadership focused on what was best for policyholders and staff."
Dan Meylink, Chief Lending Solutions Officer, Cuna Mutual Group (Ret.)

"Open and honest relationships helped everyone reach their full potential."
Mike Daubs, Chief Investment Officer, Cuna Mutual Group (Ret.)

"How Irv, a Rotarian for over 36 years, applied the Rotary motto of Service
above Self to a business crisis is inspiring. His story is a must read for ever
Rotarian."
Gary L. Whiting, Centennial District Governor 2004-05
Arizona District 5510, Rotary International

"Winning Without Greed is truly a corporate success story; one worthy of a broad audience not only in the business sector but also in the world of higher education. Burling's insights in moving an institution forward in a changing environment are highly relevant for the environment of higher education today."

Jack R. Ohle
President, Wartburg College

"Irv Burling's book offers a breath of fresh air in the world of business leadership. As a former governor and a former CEO of a major insurance company, I appreciate the contribution his book makes to our understanding of effective leadership in the changing world in both government and the corporate world."

Robert D. Ray, Governor of Iowa 1969-1983

"Irv Burling's story is one that has valuable lessons for anyone interested in ethical leadership. He tells it from a personal point of view that helps the reader see that with the appropriate moral compass one can create a 'win-win' situation that is equally beneficial to the individual, the company, and the community."

Terry E. Branstad
President, Des Moines University, Governor of Iowa, 1983-1999

WINNING
WITHOUT
GREED

IRV BURLING

Evergreen
PRESS

ISBN -1-58169-221-8
For Worldwide Distribution
Printed in the U.S.A.

Evergreen Press
P.O. Box 191540 • Mobile, AL 36619
800-367-8203

*While the situations described in this book
are real, the names of individuals are fictitious to protect
their privacy.*

TABLE OF CONTENTS

DEDICATION

*To my wife Marian who, by example,
has demonstrated the power
of building life-giving relationships
with others.
In the words of a friend, who had recently
visited our home,
"The dance you two do is filled with
extravagant loving and delight in living. It's
enveloping and encouraging, warm and vital."*

ACKNOWLEDGMENTS

I am deeply indebted to all of the editing and critiquing Fred Waldstein did on this book. When I began writing this book, I was unsure as to the help I was seeking. Nor did I know how long it would take or if I would follow it through to completion. Fred was always encouraging and motivating to the end. I appreciate the articulate way he can express himself in simple, direct terms using a minimum of words.

Every business develops its own vocabulary. It was very helpful that Fred was not a part of our business. His penetrating questions for clarification were invaluable resulting in a better end product.

Fred is Director of the Institute for Leadership Education, Professor of Political Science, and holds the endowed Irving R. Burling Chair in Leadership at Wartburg College in Waverly, Iowa.

I also want to thank Bill Withers from Wartburg College for his continuing encouragement to write this 2nd edition. His e-mails, always starting with with the word "awesome," were a continuous message to press on and very motivating. I'm honored by his words in the Foreword and Introduction. Bill is the Chair of the Communications Art Department at Wartburg.

A warm thanks to the Reverend Dr. Jerry Folk who wrote the questions at the end of the book. He is a bright articulate theologian and teacher and was most generous with his time and talent in writing a succinct thought provoking set of questions that can be used in any classroom or study group. Thank you, my friend.

I am grateful for the many individuals who had an impact on my life during my faith journey: First of all my parents, Ray and Kathryn, and the role they played in bringing me to my first church, East Union, in Carver Minnesota; friends at Woodlake in Minneapolis; Redeemer in Waverly, Iowa; Long Lake in Birchwood, Wisconsin; and Holy Trinity in Chandler, Arizona. You nurtured my soul.

I've had the privilege of sharing Rotary with Rotarians in Iowa, Wisconsin and Arizona. Rotary is made up of many common individuals who collectively accomplish extraordinary results in meeting humanitarian needs worldwide. I'd be remiss if I didn't say thank you my friends for the opportunity of joining you for more than 36 years in those life-giving endeavors.

FOREWORD

"I have someone you should meet." That was the basic invitation by my colleague here at the Wartburg College Institute for Leadership Education to meet Irving Burling at an international business conference in Honolulu. Irv was presenting ideas based on his years of work in the insurance industry, and my colleague had inquired about whether I would be willing to join their panel discussion centered around the topic of leadership, organizational change, and change management. Hawaii? My colleague didn't need to ask twice.

Throughout my years in business, and later as I decided to enter the college classroom, I've been blessed to read, conference with, and even meet some of the great leadership thinkers and writers of the 21st Century; Deming, Greenleaf, Covey, Blanchard, DePree, and Autry all come to mind. Having lived and worked in the same community that Irv Burling's company conducted commerce allowed me an awareness of his almost "urban legend" quality at times, but we had never met.

I remember seeing Irv that first time in Hawaii, not fully aware of what Parkinson's disease was or how it affects the human condition. I was waiting in the lobby of the conference center hotel in Waikiki. As I watched, he and his lovely wife, Marian, come off the elevator and walk slowly across the lobby. I remember my first thoughts were, *Certainly, this can't be the same former president and CEO who spent almost two decades leading a major, national insurance company. This isn't the man who helped transform two companies, a college, a seminary, and the lives of hundreds, perhaps thousands. This can't be the same man who changed both language and culture in a company so that all employees thought of themselves as associates and a merger was thought of as a mere permanent affiliation.*

I was wrong. This was the man—Irving Burling. And my own sense of organizational leadership and change management has never been the same since that day.

Parkinson's impacts various parts of the body, causing stiffness of muscles, slowness, and tremors. Those with Parkinson's may experience difficulty walking, talking, or completing seemingly simple tasks. The disease is both chronic, meaning it persists over a long period of time, and progressive, as its symptoms tend to worsen over time.

I quickly learned that Irving Burling has approached this disease in the latter part of his life with the same passion, persistence, and conviction that he employed as the CEO of Century Life of America, later CUNA Mutual Life Insurance Company. Today, he has entered into his own permanent affiliation with the disease, but he has not allowed it to detract him from serving and coaching others, even in these sometimes turbulent times of his own final years. In the words of Fuller Seminary's Dr. J. Robert Clinton, Irving Burling is "finishing well."

Many of us upon reaching retirement age, even those of us who claim to be Christian leaders, will succumb to our own leadership diseases. Instead of continuing to serve others, we will parachute our lives into bouts with lethargy, atrophy, or temptations and vices that are either active or latent from our more vital and productive years. Ironically, many leaders have historically not finished well. Dr. Clinton, in his own scholarly research of biblical leaders, found that only one-third of all leaders during biblical times actually finished well. I doubt we have to look much beyond our 21st Century churches or corporations to realize that this number isn't much better today.

Irving Burling is finishing well, and I am a better leader, teacher, husband, father, and friend for having known him.

The apostle Paul, in Philippians 3, captured the essence of leading beyond what we might normally think of success and counseled us instead toward continuing the journey of service toward significance. He wrote,

Not that I have already obtained all this, or have already arrived at my goal, but I press on to take hold of that for which Christ Jesus took hold of me. Brothers and sisters, I do not consider myself yet to have taken hold of it. But one thing I do: Forgetting what is behind and straining toward what is ahead, I press on toward the goal to win the prize for which God has called me heavenward in Christ Jesus. All of us, then, who are mature should take such a view of things. And if on some point you think differently, that too God will make clear to you.

After our work together at that conference, and later as he and Marian graciously allowed me into their lives—dare I say ministries—I became convicted that his was a story worth sharing.

One thing always puzzled me about those who have written and lectured around the topic of leadership, and specifically servant-leadership. Who among these great leaders, thinkers, and writers has actually done it? Show me leaders who lived it! Who among them has actually chronicled transformational, systemic change over years; no, decades? Very few.

Irving Burling's story is an impactful case history of servant-leadership that not even he fully comprehended at times. His former company is now approaching the 15th anniversary of the merger he renamed and helped lead through serving. Perhaps the better question is, how do you share such a compelling and heart-warming story with the insurance industry as a backdrop? After all, this wasn't General Electric, and Irv Burling is no Jack Welch! Welch's book is about "Winning" while Irv's is about "Winning Without Greed." No, this quickly became a story about a gentle, servant-leader with a heart for people at all levels of the organization, and it required a different format.

What better way to introduce you to Irv than through his own memoirs, his recollections on leadership during his company's—and an industry's—turbulent transformation. Whether you work in the insurance industry or volunteer at the local church, I believe you will find this story and his "corporate notes" speaking to you in ways from which I too have benefited.

As the great C.S. Lewis once wrote, "Literature adds to reality, it does not simply describe it. It enriches the necessary competencies that daily life requires and provides; and in this respect, it irrigates the deserts that our lives have already become." Is your life or leadership at work a desert?

If you or your organization are struggling through turbulent times, or as I sometimes refer to it, "permanent whitewater," or you long for a different way of thinking about working, serving, or leading...I have someone you should meet.

—*Bill Withers*
Wartburg College

INTRODUCTION

WorldCom/MCI, Waste Management, Sunbeam, Enron, Global Crossing, Arthur Andersen LLP, Tyco.... The list is staggering, at times even interconnected, and it seemingly grows each time you pick up the newspaper. Among both private and public, profit and non-profit, worker, investor, and volunteer confidence, and trust, is being betrayed. It has reached such staggering proportions among publicly traded companies in the last decade that Congress passed the Sarbanes-Oxley Act. This legislation attempts to account for the conduct of those who are supposed to be stewards of corporate accountability and governance. And yet, the leadership crisis in America is certainly not new to the headlines. The Ames brothers mired themselves in one of the country's largest financial scandals of its day with their own mismanagement and leadership crimes with the Union Pacific Railroad back in 1869.

Organizational leaders, many driven quite simply by greed, have put hundreds of thousands of employees on the street, and mergers and downsizings have swelled the ranks of those who no longer believe in organizational leaders.

And yet there appears to be a movement where leaders and followers alike are beginning to ask, "Isn't there a better way?" Even larger companies like Southwest Airlines, Herman Miller, Toro, The Vanguard Group, Men's Warehouse, and Starbucks have begun a journey into the management philosophy referred to as servant-leadership. This management approach differs from others by discarding more traditional top-down, hierarchical leadership traps, and instead emphasizes collaboration, trust, empathy, and the ethical use of influence. Greed, power, and personal gain are not a part of the equation. At heart, the organizational leader adopting this philosophy is one who wishes to serve others first.

It must be acknowledged that the concept of servant-leadership is not new. The philosophy is over 2000 years old and is commonly credited as one of the core tenants of the Christian faith. It was Jesus who many believe modeled the perfect example of a servant-leader. Throughout the scriptures it is Jesus Christ who continually encourages and even commands his followers to be more concerned for others than themselves. In Mark 8:35 and 9:35 he challenges followers to lose their lives (in service to him and others) in order to find fulfillment and meaning. Jesus' modeling of servant-leadership is the antithesis of greed, power, and personal gain.

For 30 years Irving Burling carried a three-by-five recipe card to work in his front shirt pocket. One side of the card usually featured his daily or weekly "to do list." The reverse side, however, held close to his heart for three decades, daily featured this four-word hierarchy of personal priorities: "faith, family, friends, work." He claimed as his core principles the words found in Micah 6:8. "He has showed you, O man, what is good. And what does the Lord require of you? To act justly and to love mercy and to walk humbly with your God."

In an attempt to burn this verse into his consciousness, Irv has put three words—integrity, empathy, humility—on his computer screen to remind him hourly of the message of Micah 6:8. It is how you win without greed and lead through serving others.

Because of the speed and pervasiveness of change in our culture through globalization, the proliferation of technology, and the degeneration of core values, and the way in which organizations respond to this change, we must continue to look for ways to better understand and develop effective leadership, servant-leadership.

Pastor Rick Warren often states about his

record-setting best-seller, *The Purpose-Driven Life,* "There's not a single new idea in this book." The same must be said of *Winning Without Greed.* But, this book can make a significant contribution to the servant-leader in each of us. It chronicles not only a corporate success story but also gives an intimate glimpse into the life of a Christian servant-leader through his story-telling and personal memoirs. As you will note, the last chapter is to be written by you, crafted around questions that will help you reconsider and reframe who you are and where you work and serve.

—*Bill Withers*
Wartburg College

Chapter One

Greed Creates Turbulent Times

The results of corporate greed and misman-agement surround us and have become an all too familiar part of the daily "business beat" reported by the media. Because of the mis-management of a few, many employees' lives are needlessly turned upside down and stockholders nearing retirement age are scrambling to replace their future income from stocks that have fallen drastically.

Our business and management leaders need to refocus their thinking from "What's in it for me?" to "What are my responsibilities to my customer and my employees as well as to my board of directors?"

This orientation is linked to the term, "servant-leadership," first used in 1970 by a retired businessman, Robert K. Greenleaf, in his publication, *The Servant as Leader.* Greenleaf's vision of servant-leadership is "a model that puts serving others-including employees, customers, and community-as the number one priority. Servant-leadership emphasizes increased service to others, a holistic approach to work, promoting a sense of community, and the sharing of power in decision-making."[1]

The principles and values of servant-leadership in corporations are desperately needed. It is more critical than ever before in our nation's history for business leaders to find creative ways to address the corporation's problems while providing as much job security as possible for the people who depend on them. This book focuses on the lessons that can be learned as a result of a dedicated group of individuals doing the common thing uncommonly well.

I spent more than 50 years in the insurance business. During the last 17 years of my active career I was the CEO of Century Life of America, a life insurance company where I had the opportunity to be the catalyst in transforming the company from certain demise to a sustainable future.

My 17 years as CEO began in a period of relative calm in the insurance business and ended during a period of intense competition as we approached the 21st century. It was apparent to me that the leadership skills that built the business during its first 100 years of ITS existence were different from what would be needed to survive and build a sustainable future.

During that time, large companies began a consolidation process through mergers. Small companies were not exempt from this transition, but saw they needed to reach out to other small ones in order to survive. The final means to the end of a successful transformation had to be some type of merger. However, 70% of the mergers negotiated in this country fail to meet expectations. We had to find a way to beat those odds.

"Mergers Seldom Pay Off" an article published on April 30, 2001 in the *Arizona Republic*, was based on a study done by the *Chicago Tribune* in conjunction with the consulting firm of A.T. Kearney. Some of the findings were as follows:

• Nearly seven in ten surviving companies lagged their industry peers in performance two years after the deals were completed, some dramatically.

3

- Even as the latest wave of deals transformed the corporate landscape and disrupted many lives, it failed to generate the promised returns.

- Many deals look good on paper but wither as vastly different organizational cultures, distribution channels and personal agendas surface.

In the 1990s there were roughly 46,000 mergers, which means that 32,000 failed to meet expectations! Can the probability of success be enhanced? The answer may very well be "yes." The following story describes one of the types of changes needed in the business culture for a successful merger to take place.

From the Corporate Notebook

THE FIRST SHALL BE LAST

The first company convention that was scheduled after I became CEO was held in Boyne Highlands, Michigan. These national conventions were not held every year, and I had never been to a prior one. Agents qualified to attend if they met a certain level of production, and their spouses were invited but had to pay their own expenses. There were about 500 in attendance.

Normally the board of directors met two days before the national meeting started. The first day of the meeting the board would conduct their agenda. The second day was used for relaxing and golfing before the agents and their spouses arrived. The board had always been provided with a hospitality room as a gathering place.

The opening evening of the convention was scheduled as a buffet dinner. The official meeting did not start until the next day. Before dinner the board had played golf and relaxed in the hospitality room. When I was asked by the staff in charge of the dinner to give them the names of those who would be at the head table, I replied,

"In a servant-led organization the first shall be last. There is no head table."

It never occurred to me that I needed to explain to the board members who stayed for the dinner that there would be no head table. I was naïve. Therefore some of the board members came to the dinner expecting to be waited on and demanded service from the resort staff. The bickering continued until some of the resort staff became upset enough to call the manager. They resolved the issue by serving the meal to the board but having no head table.

This problem created a noticeable buzz among the group as the guests were going through the buffet line. I missed the disruption because I was at the end of the line. After the dinner, one of the board members involved came to my room to discuss and defend their action. After about an hour of dialogue that accomplished nothing, I said I would be in his office the first day after the convention to resolve the issue.

The next morning when we began the convention, I was the first speaker. After the introduction by the emcee, the 500 agents and their spouses stood up and applauded for at least five minutes. It was hard to get them to quit. It was obvious that the attendees were sending a message to the board members, who were sitting in the back of the room, that they supported me and what I had done. This may appear to be a minor issue, but it was a major statement regarding the future direction of the company.

I told the entire board that all issues should be on the table in a transparent organization. Therefore, on the first day back at the office, I flew directly to the home of the chairman of the board to deal with the problem that the convention had unearthed. My objective was to talk through the issue, which had been uncomfortable for the board members, and to suggest a solution. I proposed that at all conventions in the future only the board chairman would be invited for the opening dinner and that there would be no board meetings held in connection with conventions.

There was a risk in making this trip. My tenure as CEO could be ended after only a matter of months at the helm, but I promised the board that they had an opportunity after every meeting to fire me if they didn't like what was happening. My objective was to be a servant leader and I expected the board to do what they could to be supportive of my position.

How the issue was dealt with must have made a powerful impression on the board member who came to my room that evening in Michigan. At his retirement years later, he met with me privately and said, holding back the tears, "You had good reason to be mad at me after Boyne Highlands, but you never showed it. Thank you."

The first step in the organizational transformation was painful and awkward but the birth of a servant-led organization occurred that Sunday evening the summer of 1976.

What I learned about the strengths or traits that helped me the most in my efforts to be a servant leader:

1. **Transparency**: What I did was as important as what I said. Standing at the end of the line created an image that the organization would not forget. The disruption actually turned into a positive statement.

2. **Integrity**: Open, honest, and timely communications was important. Dealing with an awkward situation promptly kept issues "on the table" and minimized the potential negative impact on productivity.

Questions to consider if you want to be a servant leader:

1. If you are a leader in a business what image does your staff project?

2. What image do you want to project?

3. What steps need to be taken to make the change?

---

[1] Greenleaf, R. K. 1970. *The Servant as Leader*, Indianapolis, IN: The Robert Greenleaf Center.

Chapter Two

RAFTING IN A
WHITEWATER WORLD

C entury Life of America was a small life insurance company located in the heartland
of America. It was the stable, anchor business in Waverly, Iowa, a community of 8,000. The
company's 100-year history in rural America with
its inherent work ethic had produced a very competitive, financially strong, well-respected insurance organization. Turnover was unusually low
among the employees, and never in the history of
the company had there been an early retirement. It
used to be said that when the parents of high school
graduates wished the best for their children, they

wanted them to work for the company. Recruiting was never a problem.

We called our employees "associates." When I first became CEO I would spend part of every day walking around and chatting with them. I thought I was with a company that would practically run itself for the next 100 years. What would I do with my time? Was I wrong!

The history of the insurance business is punctuated with various price wars in specific products, such as term insurance, to establish inroads in market share, but these typically never lasted more than six months. Afterwards, the pricing of products would return to what had been normal for many years. The principle of pricing products for a stable economic environment had been built into the strategic planning models of insurance companies for many years.

The fundamental foundation of most life insurance companies in this country was fashioned from life insurance that had long-term guarantees, which meant conservative interest assumptions and life expectancies involving several generations. Furthermore, to increase sales of their products, companies built commission schedules into the pricing of products, which increased expenses faster than revenue was earned. A typical insurance product did not increase company income for 10-15 years and so surplus money was used in order to write the policy.

Alliances

The relationship of the three parties in an insurance contract—the company, the agent and the client—were dependent on one another. During the first 100 years of the life insurance business in this country, however, there was a close alliance between the company and the agent. Because of the long-term nature of the product, the client didn't always understand the details of their policies except to know they were necessary to procure and the companies could be depended upon to keep their promises. The three relationships remained solid and in place. The first 100 years of the company were what I call "the comfort zone" period for the insurance business.

But the spike in interest rates in the early 80s changed all that. The consumer's primary focus became asset accumulation products with insurance playing a secondary role of completing the consumer's long-term goal in the event of a premature catastrophe.

At that point the client was saying, "I didn't understand all the guarantees and other aspects in the life insurance contract, but I understand interest rates and I want the best deal." Life insurance products lost some of their glamor, and the client demanded a new set of interest sensitive products which were innovative, had a short shelf life, and were expensive to administer. We found ourselves in a financial services war. The comfort zone had passed, and we were in a veritable war zone. The insurance business would never be the same again.

The unwritten close alliance between the company and the agent switched to one between the agent and the client. To satisfy the client's demands, the agent frequently transferred the business to another company in order to maintain their alliance with the client and retain his/her commission income. Some of the business was transferred before it had been on the books of the originating company for ten years. This meant that surplus borrowed to write the business originally was never going to be repaid.

In addition, interest sensitive products, such as annuities and universal life, meant competition from financial intermediaries outside the insurance business, such as banks and investment brokers.

The nature of these changes demanded improved technology, which was expensive. And regulators, in an attempt to stay on top of all the dramatic changes, imposed more regulations, which added to costs.

I remember going to insurance trade association meetings during the early years of the "war" and seeing my peers concerned about losing control of their company's destiny. Not only were agents transferring business to other companies, but while interest rates were so high, banks were telling their clients, "If you have a life insurance product, you're better off borrowing against it since the guaranteed rate is so low." The result was an erosion of the financial underpinnings of life insurance companies.

For 100 years insurance companies had been known as strong financial intermediaries in this country. With a stable, predictable source of income, insurance companies were making long-term investment commitments on behalf of the policyholders. These investments were a source of revenue to provide long-term financing to build businesses, homes, apartments, hotels, and infrastructure in this country. At the peak of the insurance war, demands for cash from the policyholders were exceeding cash reserves, and some companies had to go to the banks for temporary help.

14

Truly this was an entirely new ball game. The rules had changed. The higher volume of business in interest-sensitive products, which were more subject to the whims of the policyholders, meant that companies had to be more careful in making long-term investment commitments.

While I continued to build relationships of trust with associates, my thoughts were totally different than in the past. Now I was wondering, *Why is this happening to me? How does this parochial company survive in this environment? What kind of critical mass or size is needed to survive? Is it possible that we could lose a significant piece of the distribution system since loyalty meant little in this war? What happens to the associates that can't keep up?*

I'd look at the associates and say to myself, *These people and their families are counting on the business to stay in this community and not only survive but to thrive.* It weighed heavily on my conscience.

As I looked to the future I felt we had three options: 1) maintain the status quo, 2) position the company by spreading the resources in such a manner that the company would be in position to provide any financial product through any distribution system that policyholders would demand in the future, or 3) focus on a few strengths with the objective to become one of the best in a chosen market.

Maintain the Status Quo

I could have masked what was happening in our company and held on until my retirement. For example, one possibility considered by companies during this period was to sell their home office building and lease it back, and then add the value of the building to their surplus, making their company look better on paper. Another strategy involved surplus and liabilities. As a company we were always conservative in establishing liabilities, but we could have revalued those liabilities and added the extra amount to surplus, again making the company look better on paper. Furthermore, while the erosion in surplus was real, it would not have been noticeable for several years.

But masking the financial results would have violated the values and principles of openness and honesty that were at the core of our organization. For example, we had implemented an audit system using what was then one of the big eight accounting firms that had no other involvement with the company (similar to legislation implemented after the Enron travesty). We did this years before mutual insurance companies were even required to have an outside auditor. Several years before state regulators required it, we had made it a regular practice to furnish the board of directors with detailed information about the company. We wanted to make sure everything was on the table for everyone to see. In other words, we wanted to be a totally transparent organization to the 300,000 plus policyholders that entrusted their resources with us. These people had to be our first priority.

Another possibility would have been to wait and consider a traditional merger with a larger company. Typically that would eventually mean all the business would be administered at the larger company's office, and most of our staff would be forced to look for new jobs. There would be a high probability that the office would have limited use in the surviving company, producing a significant negative impact on our staff and the community.

Position the Company

I felt we needed to be more creative and, most importantly, I knew we could do better for our policyholders than a merger would have allowed. This meant that we would utilize our resources to be ready for any eventuality—any type of distribution system or product offerings—and not be a specialist in any. This would require considering, for example, the possibility of distributing our products through department stores or banks to their customers. It would also mean trying to predict which products (e.g., term insurance, disability insurance, long-term care insurance, whole life, annuities, or something entirely new) would be the hot product of the future. It was obvious that to be able to offer everything to everyone we would have to spread ourselves too thin in light of our financial underpinnings.

As a result, I felt we needed to choose an option where we would have the opportunity to be a major force in a niche market. The margins in an insurance company's annuity products were not sufficient, on their own, to support the distribution systems that insurance companies had in place. We concluded that we would have to sell off some of our smaller lines of business and focus our resources on a few product lines where we could be a significant player in the marketplace.

In Thomas Friedman's book, *The Lexus and the Olive Tree,* he refers to the new environment where there will be a tendency for the "Winners to take all" in the market. He believes the giants in the business and the companies who already hold a strong market identity would take over the market.

I saw, however, that if we positioned ourselves in a target market where we could reduce our distribution cost per sale and our administrative costs along with obtaining a greater volume, we would have an opportunity to build a sustainable future. The challenge would be to identify how to utilize that principle in our future.

If we positioned ourselves in a target market where we could reduce our distribution cost per sale and our administrative costs along with obtaining a greater volume, we would have an opportunity to build a sustainable future.

A New Day

During this time rural America was struggling. You could see it in the number of businesses closed on Main Street in the small communities. The business leaders of our community formed an economic development group to be pro-active to stop the bleeding. I was named chairman, which created additional pressure for the company to lead in a community transformation effort.

Change is difficult and scary for everyone involved. Small businesses were closing, unemployment was rising, and the anchor company in the community for the first time in its history laid off staff. People in the community understandably were nervous. On one occasion eggs were thrown at my car. There were even threats to my security. One community leader sent a letter to our Board of Directors complaining that I was out to destroy a beautiful company and the whole community. And during the height of the stress and heavy schedule, I had a mild heart attack.

The comfort zone of the first 100 years was over not only for the company but the community as well. While I had been working on methods to improve productivity in the company in my early years as CEO, there was now a high degree of urgency to implement our future strategies. My calendar became a 24/7 effort to transform the company.

From the Corporate Notebook

TRADING SPACES

Before I was the CEO I was named Executive VP and elected to the board. In that capacity I worked on special projects directly with the board.

One of the first projects I worked on was a revision of the pension plan for the home office staff. Our meetings usually were held in Chicago at a downtown club. The typical schedule was to start with a social hour, follow with dinner and then start our meeting. The meeting would be finished the following morning. At this particular meeting I had retained a professional actuary from Atlanta to provide an "outside" analysis.

The CEO, my predecessor at the time, and one of the board members had a habit of getting into an argument over systemic issues. At this particular meeting the argument, which had started during dinner, carried over into the meeting. I was frustrated because the company was paying the consultant for his time and the clock was running while the argument continued over an irrelevant issue.

Finally after an hour of argument during which we had gotten nowhere with the agenda, one of the board members asked if I had an opinion. I said, "Let me pause before I say something that I would regret for years to come." After about a three-minute delay, which seemed like an eternity, I said, "Let's get to the agenda because the company is paying for this consultant." We returned to the agenda and the next morning the board member apologized to me privately. The point is that in a transparent management style it should be self-evident that productivity starts at the top.

Just prior to becoming CEO, I was in Atlanta meeting with our consultant and a member of a consulting firm who had a national reputation in the insurance business. We were discussing the above experience and talked about what I could do that would illustrate the type of management I wanted to shape the future. The industry expert suggested that I think of something that would be dramatic and make a statement to the staff and community.

We were going to commence building a new building in a few months since we had outgrown our old office. We began discussing the possibilities of using that opportunity to define what I meant by a transparent servant-led organization. As a result we made a series of changes:

1. Instead of meeting in Chicago we met in our hometown or at the airport of a major city. Meetings were three hours long, and we tried to schedule them so members could fly in and out the same day. There was no scheduled dinner or meeting the night before. The net result of this change saved the company over $25,000 a year. We did have an occasional resort meeting, but board members paid their own way.

2. We used what is called a design/build operation to construct the home office. This process saved a lot of time and money. My point was that we were in the insurance business not the construction business.

3. The old home office had a long rectangular board table with the chairman seated at the head of the table. The room was traditionally used only for board meetings. In the new office we had a round table and the room was used extensively by the staff. The objective was to illustrate that we were all in this together.

4. In the old board room there was a cabinet that held wine and cigars. After each board

meeting, members would relax with a glass of wine and a cigar. When I was asked where the cabinet should be put in the new office, I said, "We won't be needing it. Sell it."

5. When I was asked about the design for the executive bathroom since the old office had one, I said, "We don't need it."

6. We eliminated all bells that had been used for years to designate lunch and coffee breaks. The future was to be built on mutual trust.

7. There was no chair across from my desk but a round table where we could mutually discuss issues.

8. All interior walls of offices were either glass or open cubicles symbolizing openness to all with no hidden agendas or meetings held behind closed doors.

At the first meeting at which I was named CEO, I was asked for some comments. I said, "What we've created in this office is an illustration of the transparent management style that I want to follow. I pledge to you to always have all the issues laid out on the table, and I expect you to do the same."

The objective in all these changes reminds me of a statement by Emerson: "What you are speaks so loudly I can't hear what you're saying."

What I learned about strengths or traits that helped me the most in my efforts to be a servant leader:

1. Integrity: What you do should be consistent with what you say. Setting an example of what you expect is important. If you're asking your staff to focus on productivity and a control of expenses it should be obvious that you're doing it too.

2. Transparency: It is important that your physical surroundings represent an image of what you say. It made a huge statement when the long board's table was replaced with a round one. Glass walls, including my own office, projected an open image. When a visiting consultant from Boston walked in the door, he said, "I knew I was in the right office!"

Questions to consider if you want to be a servant leader:

1. What kind of an image do you create as a leader?

2. What image do you want to create?

3. How can you change it?

4. Do you want to change?

Chapter Three

BECOMING LEAN TO SURVIVE

We did not have the economies of scale needed to offset the rising cost of doing business. For years we had tried to increase the number of new policies written in one year to exceed 30,000 but were consistently unsuccessful. Our experience followed the national trend—we had about a 2% drop in life insurance policies written each year and about a 6% increase in annuities. Furthermore, to aggravate the problem, the margins on annuities could not support our distribution system, and there were ominous signs that there would be no improvement in the foreseeable future.

For the long term good of the organization, we needed to form a partnership with another company. Finding the right partner for a long-term fit and preparing our associates for the major changes the partnership would entail would take time. Furthermore, to avoid a gradual erosion of the strength of the company, we needed to stop the hemorrhaging right away. I had to immediately cut expenses and assemble a group of associates who were much more pro-active in building a sustainable future.

The changes we needed to make would be traumatic. The company had never experienced a general lay-off or early retirement in more than 100 years. Some of the terminations would involve my best friends. The trust we had worked so hard to build would suffer.

We did a number of things to help in the transition:

- At our monthly meetings with the entire staff, we spelled out the problem. On a huge chart we showed the trend over the last several years of the ratio of expenses to premium income. It was approaching 14% and for the type of business we were writing, it

28

should have been less than 10%. We indicated that we were working on ways to increase premiums. We asked everyone to look for ways to cut expenses.

• We held a session for senior officers to address issues such as, "How do we practically communicate the change? What should we expect? How do we react?" The discussions and dialogue we had were invaluable because we were able to deal with the staff's reactions promptly and constructively.

• The first step we took was to offer early retirement for those individuals over a certain age. The incentive package we offered made it attractive for about ten associates, and we did not replace them.

• We sold off minor lines of business, eliminated some functions that we felt we could do without in a crunch, and expanded the responsibilities of some managers so we ended up having fewer managers, but with each one managing more associates. This eliminated almost 1/4 of the staff. To help the associates who left the company, we offered a generous severance package—the longer the service,

the greater the severance—and provided professional placement services to help them in
the transition.

- There is a limit on how much you can
downsize an organization without hurting
the core of its operation. Any further cuts
would have to be temporary until we found a
way to increase premiums. After three years
and cutting 1/4 of the associates, we still had
not reached the 10% ratio we were striving to
achieve.

I'll never forget the year-end budget meeting we
held, trying to determine where we could cut eight
more positions. I suggested to the senior officers
that we sleep on it and resolve the problem the first
thing in the morning.

When I returned to my desk there was a letter
from the state of Washington for a $50,000 assess-
ment! The states operate state guarantee associa-
tions so if a company licensed in the state goes
bankrupt, the state assesses each company licensed
in the state a sufficient amount so in total the policyholders are made whole and one of the domestic
companies takes over the management. In effect we
were covering for some company that had for years

refused to make the hard decisions. The next morning I reluctantly had to announce to our senior officers that we had to cut ten positions not eight.

We cut 10 positions, picking those who had the smallest impact on achieving our objective of a 10% ratio. The associates who remained with the company understood the issue and knew that we were willing to face the tough problem. I also felt that they knew we were trying hard to find a way to increase premiums.

It was a time of challenge for our company, but we were able to use these challenges to make our company a stronger one overall. Although we had to cut some positions, it was only as a last resort with the end view to create a stable work environment for the remaining employees. We used the assessments of the individuals to identify those who really did not fit either with the new company profile or with the assignments their job entailed. Some of their stories follows.

From the Corporate Notebook

BUILDING ON OUR STRENGTHS

When I received the first invitation to join the company, I turned it down because I wasn't convinced they were committed to any long term objective but rather to simply maintaining the status quo. Six months later, they asked me if I would reconsider. I suggested that the first step would be to have an independent industrial psychologist do a vocational evaluation assessment to see whether or not my strengths matched what the company needed.

The company agreed and made the necessary arrangements for an independent assessment. The net result of the assessment was that I appeared to be a good match for the company in Waverly. I then asked that some of the board members read the report and discuss it with me. After completing this process, I agreed to move.

From that point on I was convinced that we needed to use of vocational assessments to help employees reach their ultimate potential. Since then I have been accused of being too dependent on assessments, but one of the keys to developing effective leaders is accurate self-knowledge. It's an excellent tool to help individuals focus on their strengths.

Because I was dealing with the company's most important asset, I went to great lengths to have good development plans. Periodically I would do my own personal assessment of individuals reporting to me, take the information to Minneapolis to discuss it with a professional who had additional information, and then summarize possible development plans for the staff member.

For more than 100 years the company had been a very effective process-driven organization, making sure that processes were done right. When the market is demanding rapid changes, the primary focus must first be on making sure you're doing the right thing. Warren Bennis, who wrote *On Becoming a Leader,* stated that leaders master the context of what they face, whereas managers surrender to the context. If an individual was overwhelmed with the changes he or she faced, I used assessments to outsource them to jobs in other companies for better utilization of their strengths. Let me give a couple of examples.

I wanted to keep one of the individuals because he was bright, had a broad background, and was articulate. He, however, had an attitude that was fundamentally different from the direction the company was going. I asked my coach to sit down with the two of us and serve as a mediator. After extensive discussions we decided that the relationship was unworkable. We used the same source to help this individual find a new job where he was better suited, and we remained friends.

Two individuals were struggling with assignments. Their assessments indicated that they would be unhappy in the future, and the individuals reluctantly agreed with the assessment. In addition to being more market-driven, we were becoming a servant-led organization. I had an independent executive consultant attend some group meetings on the changes we were facing and offered couples the opportunity for private sessions. The individuals received assessment help to get new jobs, and we continued to be on pleasant speaking terms.

I received a call from a peer of mine running another company. He had heard of my use of assessments and asked me if I would use the resource I had to do an assessment on a candidate for a new job in his company. I agreed. The final report indicated that the candidate was not a good match for the job being considered. The CEO of the other company responded that there must be some mistake. I challenged the professional, but after thorough reexamination the report seemed appropriate. The CEO decided to ignore the recommendation and hired the individual. Several years later the individual failed in the assignment. While I was at times accused of being too dependent on assessments, it was very obvious that if the CEO had listened to this particular report, he would have saved the individual's career. By not listening, this individual's career was ruined.

I endorse Warren Bennis's comment that self-knowledge is one of the fundamentals in the development of leaders. When an industrial psychologist came to the office, I spent time with him, and the insights we exchanged were a valuable resource in leading the company. In fact I retained one personally to do an assessment on each of my three children when they were seniors in high school. It's interesting that all three have ended up in careers pointed to in their assessments without any further meddling by me.

What I learned about the strengths or traits that helped me the most in my efforts to be a servant leader:

1. **Development**: Always allocate plenty of time to agree on a development plan for each staff member. Audit the plan every year. Do a new assessment every three years. Keep the member challenged by periodically assigning increased responsibility. Beware of assigning responsibilities beyond the member's capacity to manage.

Questions to consider if you want to be a servant leader:

1. As a leader how can you improve the development plan for each individual that reports to you?

2. What issues are there with staff that I've been reluctant to deal with?

3. Are there any areas where professionals would help in the utilization of my most important asset?

4. How do I know if I'm doing the best I can do with Human Resources?

Chapter Four

MODIFYING
THE MERGER MODEL

The easiest solution to the dilemma I faced during the "war" was to merge the company and leave town. Because of the quality and history of the company, I received several unsolicited opportunities to do just that. This option may have still met the needs of the policyholders, but the best interests of our hard-working associates and the community in which most of them lived demanded the exploration of alternative options. We needed to see if there was a creative solution to the future so that everyone could be a winner in the long term. Because we were one of the early companies to react to what was happening in our business, I thought we might have more options.

After extensive searching for a partner, I finally found what seemed to be the perfect match I was seeking. The CUNA Mutual Insurance Group sold a variety of products to credit unions, and through credit unions to their members. They did not market products directly to the members of the credit union. At Century Life, however, we had the marketing and administrative expertise to sell products directly to the members of the credit union. It was a niche market for Century Life. It was a good fit.

In one of the first serious merger meetings I had with the CEO of CUNA Mutual and their consultant, the consultant was describing the merits of a merger and how this would meet the needs of both companies. It apparently was obvious to him that I was dragging my feet when he asked me, "Are we going too fast?" I replied, "I'm not interested if we're going to use a method where the professionals who work on mergers state that the probability of meeting expectations is less than 50%. We need to be more creative."

Why was I so against a traditional merger? There were several reasons.

- When you're trying to do the right thing for those you're trying to serve, in our case the policyholders, a 30% probability of meeting expectations is not a satisfactory bet for responsible management. As good stewards of our clients' resources, we ought to be able to do better than that.

- I simply didn't want our company to be swallowed up by another. In a traditional merger, one of the companies disappears and the staff of the survivor takes most of the key positions and the other company's employees are let go. The increased size of the surviving entity is intended to generate greater efficiencies and thus higher productivity. Most likely in our case, we would lose most of our associates, and the operations would probably have been moved out of town. Two things worth preserving would be lost—first, a dedicated staff that as a unit had a capacity to deliver one of the better product values available; and second, a significant economic base for the community.

• A merger tends to be "event" driven meaning that on a certain day the operations would cease in the smaller company. Obviously it is very traumatic to your greatest asset—the loyal men and women who have given so much to the company.

• In addition, the merger process tends to be driven from the "top down." I believe you can improve the chance of success of the venture by involving associates throughout the organization in the end result.

By removing the shackles of what everyone else had done for years, we were able to create our own future.

Permanent Affiliation Versus Merger

The concept of permanent affiliation versus merger could have advantages in any consolidation. For us the bottom line was that we could keep our most important asset—our human resources—intact, and we could utilize the plant we had in a location where there was an excellent employment base. By removing the shackles

40

of what everyone else had done for years, we were able to create our own future.

No matter how you cut it, the decision to downsize is a painful process. It is widely recognized that one of the challenges of leadership is to avoid taking the path of least resistance by choosing what will be popular in the short-term over long-term accountability. In our case we downsized for the long-term benefit of the owners—the clients.

This takes authentic leadership which, in the words of Ronald Heifetz, requires "adaptive work." "Adaptive work consists of the learning required to address conflicts in the values people hold, or to diminish the gap between the values people stand for and the reality they face. Adaptive work requires a change in values, beliefs, or behavior."[1] It was only through the willingness of all associates to engage in adaptive work that we were able to survive as an organization.

When we were ready to begin the transition, I was determined to not even use the word, "merger." We needed to think outside the box. I was adamant in selectively using language and any other tools that would help us think in new ways. We named the process a "permanent affiliation."

The concept of merger is so inborn in our culture that I probably corrected individuals no fewer than a hundred times: "It is not a merger!" In fact five years after completing the very successful collaborative effort, I received a cryptic note on a Christmas card from a local businessman, which simply said, "I still say it was a merger!"

The objective was to create a sustainable, more productive joint effort by building synergistically on the strengths of each organization. The essential difference between what we did and a merger was that the legal entity of the smaller company remained intact. While the name was changed for business reasons, the financials of each entity remained separate and were reported to the state regulators as such.

What impact did the permanent affiliation have on our associates? The larger company had a staff of more than 3,000 functioning as a group operation, with sales and billing done through the credit unions to the member. Our staff was fewer than 300 with marketing and administrative expertise in individual direct sales to the member. I was asked more than once, "Are you sure you know what you're doing? They will chew you up and spit you out." It never happened. For many years CUNA

Mutual had tried to provide the type of products and services we provided on an individual basis to supplement their operations for their marketplace but had not been successful. Therefore they were as interested as we were in doing what was right for the policyholders.

As mentioned earlier, we had downsized by 1/4 before I found this solution that would generate more revenue. During this process, we lost only one associate who voluntarily chose an opportunity with another company. We deliberately broadened our distribution system and number of representatives in preparation for our new affiliation.

A Successful Strategy

It proved to be a successful strategy. Currently more than 80 field and home office associates have moved into positions in the larger company, and those that remained assumed broader assignments in the smaller company. The employment base in the smaller company increased to nearly 800 from the original 300 people and is still growing.

Additional building space and new roads were needed to accommodate the growth, which of course necessitated additional support services in the community for the increased staff. In effect the community anchor company has become even stronger with a sustainable future, and in turn the community has benefited.

On a recent trip I drove through the community again after being gone for almost ten years. It was heartening to see the growth—a new highway system, a 25% growth in the student population of the local college from its lowest point, more than $30 million of new construction at the college, a number of new home development areas, an additional golf course, added motels and businesses, a new up-to-date library and plans for an expansion in the insurance office to consolidate the functions which have grown into four separate buildings.

The net change in the company is also dramatic and impressive.

• Because we are now in a target market, the cost of distribution per unit sale decreased significantly.

• The administration of the individual business previously written by the larger company plus a dramatic increase in business written under additional distribution systems meant improved productivity gains—a greater volume of business was being processed within the same facility with proportionately less staff.

• A three-fold increase in assets is now managed by one staff instead of two.

• Integration of functions has saved millions.

• Applications for policies increased from under 30,000 per year to nearly a million per year!

I remember when some of our professional underwriters returned from a National Underwriters meeting. The gossip at the meeting was how most of the companies were looking for ways to reassign their professional underwriters because business was down. We were now looking for ways to employ more because of our business had increased!

[1] *Leadership Without Easy Answers*, p.22

From the Corporate Notebook

BELIEVING IN THE CREATIVITY OF OUR ASSOCIATES

I knew that our staff had the creative capacity to accomplish the affiliation. I trusted them. I needed to focus my attention on building a team spirit. The most effective thing I did in getting the focus needed to succeed was to answer the field manager who had asked me what our back-up plan was. I said, "There is none. This must succeed."

There were a number of quotes we used during these trying days to encourage the staff. I received a letter recently from one of the senior officers, which said, "Those statements after fifteen years continue to be part of the DNA!" Following are some of those statements:

• *Assume good intentions.* This was extremely successful. When you put two cultures together that were totally different, it generated more of a spirit of collaboration than antagonism.

• *The price of perfection is prohibitive.* This was helpful in moving a process-driven culture toward a market-driven culture.

- *It's not easy, but nothing worthwhile ever is.* It's a simple statement, very self-evident, but was a useful tool many times during our deliberations.

- *It's amazing what you can accomplish when you don't care who gets the credit.* This has been used by many organizations, and we found it very useful.

- *Tell them. Then tell them again what you said. Then ask them to tell you their understanding of what you said.* This approach was extremely helpful in eliminating misunderstandings and rumors.

A bit of humorous communication happened one evening when I was giving a speech to an industry group in a neighboring city. One of the marketing officers had gone with me to the meeting. My companion stepped out of the room to go to the washroom, which was downstairs. He happened to miss a step, fell and sustained a significant bruise on his head. He was hurt enough to be taken to a local hospital for an evaluation. The doctor was suspicious of a concussion so he asked him, "Who is the President?" Instead of saying Ronald Reagan, he said Irv Burling, so they kept him overnight!

What I learned about the strengths or traits that helped me the most in my efforts to be a servant leader:

1. **Team**: Assuming good intentions, making sure communications were heard, not worrying about who gets the credit and not having a back-up plan all helped in building a cohesive team effort.

2. **Trust**: Letting the staff know I believed in them built trust.

Questions to consider if you want to be a servant leader:

1. As a leader how do you show belief in your staff?

2. How do you communicate with your staff?

3. How could you do #1 and #2 better?

4. What examples do you have to demonstrate that you're getting the results you expect?

Chapter Five

LEADERS PLAYING
IN A NEW BALLGAME

The leadership skills required to function efficiently during the "comfort zone" were different than those required to function effectively in the "war zone."

In the comfort zone, the primary emphasis was on maintaining a status quo management style with the main emphasis on improving organizational efficiency. Managers in this role tend to think of change in incremental terms. These types of managers are not well-suited for an environment which requires non-incremental change. They often become paralyzed by their need for extensive analysis and their desire for support within an organizational structure that is no longer viable. Functioning in the war zone can be extremely frustrating and debilitating for these kinds of managers.

In the war zone, the manager must always be looking for new ways to do things—past practices are not that important. The need for innovative, quick decisions means the manager must be willing to be held more accountable for the results.

I frequently have used basketball to think of the difference in management styles needed in the comfort zone versus the war zone. Basketball players today are much taller on average than they were when I played. To make it more challenging, the comfort zone manager would consider raising the height of the basket. The war zone manager, on the other hand, would consider eliminating the basket and changing the game and the rules of how you score. Clearly they are two different mind sets.

Leadership in the Comfort Zone

During my early years with the company, I worked hard to build a level of trust with the associates. For example, in the early 70s before I was named CEO, there was an attempt by the associates to organize a union to represent them in their negotiations with management. The Board of Directors asked me to represent management, and through that process, I worked closely with the head of Human Resources and managers to understand their grievances.

When I became CEO I was always available to deal with human relations problems. We regularly conducted attitude surveys, which measured the level of trust between associates and management, and took corrective action where necessary. After several years of working at this process, the outside source we used to conduct the surveys indicated that the trust level was one of the highest they had encountered.

To get an outside perspective of the company, I asked a consultant friend of mine who had been in the business for many years and worked with many different insurance companies to describe in his words the profile and culture of our company as he currently saw it. He used terms like resistant to change, methodical, reactive, paralyzed with analysis, paternalistic, a typical mutual company and parochial.

I had an independent survey done of regional

businesses and received the same statements in describing the company. In addition, I had a number of management audits done internally so I would have a good handle on not only the outside perspective, but the inside one as well.

Leadership in the War Zone

We had made progressive changes during the comfort zone time but the fact remained that we were still simply another mutual insurance company among many—strong but small among the giants and no market niche. I remember the time one of my favorite field managers from Texas said to me, "Why can't we operate like we did in the past? Let's go back to the good old days." But it would never happen anymore than there would be a resurrection of the small family farms in America.

I immediately saw that we needed:
- to cut our cost of operations
- to have a niche
- to be more proactive
- to have a clear vision of where we were headed
- to be committed to a vision with passion.

We wanted to build a sustainable future where our humanitarian interest and absolute integrity were very transparent to everyone with whom we did business. I asked myself, *What characteristics of leadership are needed to lead an organization through an extensive transformation? What skills do I have to hone in order for us to do our very best?* We could not fail in this effort if the company was to survive.

After a considerable amount of reading and listening to a number of experts on the subject, I came up with the following leadership skills and attributes I would need:

- A capacity to establish a clear vision for the future.
- The ability to be able to effectively communicate that vision.
- A very apparent willingness to listen to others when shaping a vision.
- The tenacity of a bulldog to hold onto the vision.
- A selfless attitude with minimal ego needs.

I shared this information with our board of directors and told them that these attributes must apply to all our managers and, in particular, to me. At the end of every board meeting when they would hold their executive session, I suggested the first agenda item should be: Do we continue to retain Irv as CEO? Can he continue to be the catalyst for change to transform the company into a viable business for the next century? The stakes were high. We could not fail.

Until you're faced with adversity, you don't know if you're up to the task. But at the same time, the way you deal with adversity can be a life-giving experience.

I decided to focus on the following:

• Find as compassionate a way as possible to downsize the company to stop the eroding of the company's financial underpinnings.

• Find a partner where it would be in the best interest of both companies to work together to build a sustainable future into the 21st century.

• Develop a very deliberate process so that the vision for the future became the passion for every associate.

• Hire a coach to make sure I stuck to the agenda as I've outlined.

• Create an innovative Human Resource strategy to make the most of the talent in the organization.

• Focus on our performance appraisal discipline with renewed effort at the corporate, departmental, and individual level in order to improve the climate for performance in the company.

I traveled to Philadelphia, the location of a consulting company, which was developing a technique to measure organizational productivity, to pore over the results of their surveys in which we were one of the participants. Most importantly, I reviewed my plans with the consultants to change the climate of our company, including personnel changes where necessary. We discussed in great detail my goals to implement change, going back and forth until I felt comfortable with the plan. It was extremely helpful in this process to have the independent opinion of the consultants to continually challenge my options and conclusions. It gave me a sense of being well-prepared for any course of action I took.

To keep up with the changes that we and other insurance companies were making to adapt to the changing economic environment, we held a number of meetings for virtually all levels of employees. These meetings included the following:

- Our senior officers attended a seminar in Boston on the psychology of change, understanding the psychological contract between the employees and the company, and managing an organization through such a change.

- We held a two-day seminar conducted by a guest psychologist for senior officers and their spouses on "climate for change" issues.

- Some of our junior officers attended a university course on organizational change.

- We held dinners for our managers and their spouses to talk about the changes and the reasons behind them.

- We held monthly meetings for all associates to talk about the changes and answer questions.

- At each board or committee meeting, we discussed "Organizational Renewal" and what I was anticipating for the future.

We had the advantage of an early start in creating our long-term strategy for not only surviving but sustaining the operation. And it worked!

From the Corporate Notebook

AN EDUCATION IN LEADERSHIP

For many years I wondered why I kept running into leadership challenges, which were very difficult to deal with. In fact I kept asking myself, "Why me, God?" Warren Bennis, in his book *On Becoming a Leader,* notes there is no formal education for leaders except experience. The classes in business schools are fashioned for managers.

I'd like to share with you some experiences I've had in a leadership role I've had at church for many years. While there were tough issues to deal with for which I had no experience, just when I needed a lift, God brought me moments of grace.

In the beginning I had simply been a sponsor with church youth groups in order to grow with my children. I was still busy with my education so I kept refusing requests to take on leadership roles. Within a couple of hours after receiving notice I had passed my final actuarial exam, I had a call from my pastor. He asked me to head up the stewardship drive in the fall which I agreed to do. The campaign was minimally successful, but I learned the importance of organization and follow-up on the details.

Within two months after finishing the stewardship drive I became president of the congregation. The pastor turned out to be a great mentor and a beloved friend. As congregational president, I had the responsibility for terminating two youth pastors. I learned about the extreme importance of empathy in helping individuals experiencing traumatic change in their life. I asked myself, "Why me, God?" but again I was blessed with moments of grace.

After I became CEO of the company in Iowa, I was named to the board of regents of a college. Three years later I was chairman. Shortly thereafter the college faced a crisis of a potential faculty no confidence vote on the president.

There were two fundamental problems to the issue. 1) How do you determine the truth between the faculty and the administration? and 2) how do you get a group of volunteers, the regents, to make a tough unpopular decision, if it was necessary? I asked our national church office in Minneapolis to give me the names of retired college presidents who were not in one of our church schools and who had successfully served at least 10 years.

We found an individual that met our criteria in Washington D.C. We asked him to conduct a management audit, which would give the regents a sense of the efficacy and efficiency of the current administration for the next six years, the normal term of appointment. It became apparent that the president's services must be terminated.

Immediately following the termination of this president, we started the search for another. This search happened during a period of time when demographics worked against sustaining student enrollment and turnover in college leadership was unusually high. I indicated we had to have a solution within six months or the college would suffer.

We processed more than 100 candidates and were successful in naming someone whose tenure lasted 17 years. In reporting the timely results of the search to the faculty and staff, I remember being asked if I knew the new president prior to starting the search. The underlying assumption was that because the search was completed in six months while other colleges had vacancies for more than a year, I must have managed the solution. While this man turned out to be a great president and a cherished friend, I had never heard of him before the search. So I told those who asked, "No, I never knew him before the search, but my faith in God works."

These were trying days for the college and again I asked myself, "Why me, God?" and again I was blessed with the necessary moments of grace.

Sometime later I was elected to the board of regents of a seminary in Iowa. I was the only businessman on the board; most of the members were pastors. When we received a call from the national church office in Minneapolis that the seminary was in trouble financially and would not be able to meet their payroll in two weeks, I didn't even ask the question. I knew that God would be there to help me.

Again we conducted a management audit, which I was asked to spearhead along with two individuals not connected to the seminary. The result was that I was asked by the board to advise the president that his services would be terminated. We recruited a new management team and developed a five-year plan that would restore the financial strength of the seminary. The plan was completed in four years.

Warren Bennis would say that the experiences I had provided me with an excellent education. Those experiences were invaluable when I was the catalyst for the transformation of the company into a servant-led organization with a sustainable future.

What I learned about the strengths or traits that helped me the most in my efforts to be a servant leader:
1. **Leadership**: Experiences in your work can be helpful. I also found that the many experiences I had outside of my work were extremely valuable when I had to make radical changes in the company in order for the company to have a viable future. At the time I couldn't understand why, but as I look back I realized I was very blessed with a rich education.

Questions to consider if you want to be a leader:
1. What experiences have you had that have added to your leadership education?

2. How could you apply your experiences to assume a leadership role today?

3. How could you turn the problems you face today into useful experiences for leadership roles?

From the Corporate Notebook

SERVICE ABOVE SELF

The United Way organization in our community was suffering from lack of funds because of a poor campaign during the prior year. They asked me if I would serve on the board, which was a three-year commitment. I said, "No, I don't have time for that long a commitment, but I will raise funds for you to bring your financials back in order." They agreed and I took our company communications director, whom I called a "sweeper," whose job it was to follow up on all details. The sweeper attended all interviews and meetings with me. By this time in my career, the company had developed a positive reputation in the community so I had the luxury of picking the best volunteers for the various phases of the campaign.

We were very successful. We covered the previous years debts and had plenty of funds for the following year.

Another experience I had was with some area churches that had been struggling with establishing a Habitat for Humanity organization. One neighboring county had failed, and the county I lived in had struggled for several years to get one started. A meeting was called for the purpose of examining the possibilities.

The office in Chicago for Habitat for Humanity advised that it would take about 18 months for one to be up and running. I was a stranger to most of the people at the meeting, and I had never done this before, but I volunteered to head up the effort. I told them I only had six months in which to get it done. I simply did not want to spend 18 months on one campaign. I asked for volunteers for six different divisions. I divided up the manual into six pieces and gave them to each individual and set up the first meeting to follow in a few days.

I also found a volunteer who was a wonderful "sweeper," making sure that everyone did their part in this effort. As we progressed, it looked like we would get most of it done in five months and raise enough money to start building homes in the county and in Honduras. The only thing we needed was to visit the national headquarters and they needed to visit our site. I took the entire package of our submission with our commitments to Chicago with the understanding that they would come to visit the site within two weeks. The first board meeting was held and we were up and running in six months and the neighboring county joined our forces.

What I learned about the strengths or traits that helped me the most in my efforts to be a servant leader:

1. **Leadership**: Community and business related opportunities are an excellent source for leadership training.

Questions to consider if you want to be a servant leader:

1. What opportunities are there to devote 10% of your working time to charitable endeavors that would provide an education in leadership for you?

2. What experiences have you had that have added to your leadership education?

3. How could you apply your experiences to assume a leadership role today?

Chapter Six

A SHARED VISION

The process used to create the permanent affiliation was patterned after the process we used when we built a new home office building. In building the office, we had the architect draw detailed plans for the exterior but not the interior. While the outside was being constructed, the architect then began drawing the interior. The end product was done much quicker and at a lower cost.

We used a similar model to develop the affiliation. We laid out the vision of where we wanted to be in five years, and then within given parameters, our associates began to implement the plan.

I remember one of our marketing managers saying to me, "I understand where you want the organization to be in five years, but what if it doesn't work, what is your back up plan?" I replied, "There isn't any back up plan. This must work!" This attitude had a tremendous advantage in bringing out the creative capacity of our associates.

In the insurance business, there has always been a willingness to share non-proprietary information. In this instance no one had done an affiliation before and so our staff could not benefit from the experiences of other companies. Furthermore, I had said this must work. No one ever came into my office to tell me something wouldn't work. They figured it out. They were forced to come up with a solution.

In effect the outer design was done. The internal processes were designed by those who knew the most about them. The detail of the permanent affiliation was being driven from the "bottom up." People throughout the organization were being listened to and empowered to come up with solutions.

The only way the permanent affiliation was going to be a success was if the associates could understand and adopt the vision with a passion. They had to take ownership of the vision in order to achieve a successful transformation. I'm reminded of the following story of Ozzie, one of our associates.

Ozzie's responsibilities were principally janitorial, but he also picked up visitors at the local airport, which was 15 miles from our office. One cold wintry day, he picked up a visiting consultant from Philadelphia. On the way back to the office, the consultant asked Ozzie, "What's new?" He expected to get a report on the weather but instead Ozzie said, "Year to date our premium income is up and the expense ratio is down." The consultant was shocked, and I was thrilled. The process was working. People at every level of the organization were invested in helping to shape the vision and beginning to own it.

Sharing the Vision With Associates

The number one key to accomplishing our goal was the attention given to our communications plan to share the vision with all associates. We had total commitment throughout the organization that our vision would be a reality because:

1. Our associates understood the problems the company faced.

2. We went to great lengths to communicate our vision for the future; and

3. We continually communicated our progress toward that vision.

Communication was critical in bringing all associates into the process and allowing them to develop ownership in the vision. Ownership of the process was a critical factor. This could not have been done without a very good communications plan. Furthermore, as the process of change evolved, it became increasingly apparent, as noted by Oakley and Krug in their book *Enlightened Leadership,* that "people don't resist change as much as they resist being changed." There was never any doubt in my mind that the affiliation would be accomplished. Perhaps an analogy helps explain my sense of resolve.

I've always been fond of Boston bull terriers, a special kind of bulldog. I use to play tug-of-war with one of them, using an old sock. I believe I could have walked around all day with it hanging onto that old sock until it lost all its teeth. That's the same kind of tenacity with which we held onto the vision of our strategy. When everyone understands what you're trying to do and they're all participating in the solution, your chances of success improve significantly.

Fundamental Beliefs

Before we established our vision for the future, I felt it was important to put into writing our fundamental beliefs as an organization. We spent months reviewing input from "climate for performance" studies and attitude surveys discussed at length in an earlier chapter. In addition, we reviewed input from personal interviews of residents in the area and industry representatives.

Our senior officers then spent several retreats and a number of meetings simplifying the fundamental beliefs that we wanted to hold into the next century into a few crisp statements. To emphasize the permanence of these beliefs, we printed them on granite and gave one to each associate. That piece of granite stated:

WE BELIEVE:

- Trust is earned by treating others with dignity and respect.

- Success depends on developing the abilities of our associates.

- Our associates have the creative capacity to solve problems.

- Communications should be open, honest and timely.

- Performance must be measured by long-term results.

A Three-fold Strategic Vision

The first strategy for our long-term vision for the company was to find a partner who was in a target market that would provide unlimited growth opportunities for our distribution system. With the added volume we would be able to reduce our total cost for the underwriting of new business. Second, we wanted to administer additional blocks of business currently on the books with the same plant and staff to achieve a reduction in unit costs for both companies. And third, we wanted to consolidate similar functions to reduce the duplication of effort in the two companies.

There is a lot written about keeping strategy ahead of structure. Clearly the long-term strategy for the two organizations was to be successful, albeit the most difficult to implement. There was a natural instinct to start focusing on the other two strategies, which tend to be more structural. Not only is it easier to grasp the possible changes but the results are more immediate.

The key to success for both organizations was the joint marketing and administrative capacity of the smaller company in the larger company's market. In the long term, if this were done effectively, it would generate more improvement in productivity than the consolidation of functions.

Every time someone suggested an integration of functions, I asked, "Show me how that will impact our number one strategy and our timetable for achieving it." It was my way of keeping strategy ahead of structure so that we would maximize the long-term return to the policyholders and thus sustain the permanent affiliation.

Effective Communications

The monthly, in-house bulletin board announcements and regularly scheduled meetings were not going to be sufficient to keep associates sufficiently informed because changes were happening so fast. I remember an instance when the company was making some necessary changes to the exterior of our building. Understandably it became a matter of curiosity for the community. When people would ask our associates what was happening, unfortunately they didn't have the answer. It was an illustration of how difficult it was to keep everyone informed when changes were coming so fast. We were constantly seeking new ways to help our associates to always be "in the know."

Reaching our goals was only going to happen through the combined efforts of all our associates, and they needed to have accurate and timely information. They had to own the vision. The following are some of the changes we made to help them:

• We assigned different individuals the responsibility to be an information guru. Information was disseminated as soon as needed in whatever format worked the best at the moment. I was always available when any of them needed my attention.

• We held regularly scheduled meetings to report results and laid out actions to be taken. We broke the meetings down into sufficient size to encourage questions and participation.

• In addition to my efforts to manage by walking around, I regularly table-hopped during coffee breaks and lunches to be available to answer questions and encourage dialogue and openness.

• Periodically we held meetings with community business leaders to keep them informed.

• Luncheon meetings were held with spouses of managers and retirees to keep them informed.

One of the key reasons we were successful was that we kept our associates well informed. Because they were well informed, they were in a position to contribute to the process. They were the ones who made it happen.

From the Corporate Notebook

IRVING CAN DO IT

My family would tell you that I'm always working on some problem or vision and a plan to fulfill it. I also always had a focused passion on achieving the goal. An overdone strength becomes a weakness, and I'm sure you'd find those who would say I sometimes overdo it. If what I'm doing seems right, after making sure I'm listening to what is going on around me on the subject, I adopt Churchill's message to never, never, never give up.

Ever since my children were in the early grades, I've had a tradition of having a periodic one-on-one breakfast with them to discuss their current plans. The breakfast always ended up with turning over the place mat and writing down the plan. To this day the expression "It's time to turn over the place mat" has a special meaning. I always ended those sessions with positive reinforcement, telling them, "You can do it."

Through the years I've been fortunate in having six individuals who in effect helped me by their life-giving positive reinforcement. Throughout this book I've used fictitious names (to protect the privacy of the individuals concerned), but in this one instance I'll use real names. All six have passed away. All echoed the same message of "Irving can do it."

The first time I remember hearing it was from Hildur Carlson. She was my teacher in a rural school through my first six grades. Because we lived only 1/4 mile from school, she lived with us. I can so vividly hear her say that both at school and at home. In fact I have this image of her standing over me at my desk one time as I was taking a test. I was stuck on a question and all she said was, "Irving can do it." I wrote down the answer, Sam Houston. I was right! I just didn't trust myself.

The second individual who said it was Alf Romstad. He was my pastor when I finished actuarial exams until I moved to Iowa. He didn't like to deal with tough personnel issues. I told him if he'd handle the spiritual issues, I'd deal with the tough administrative issues as president. Each term of president lasted 2 years. When my term was up, he wanted to continue to meet weekly for coffee. Those were life-giving sessions where there was mutual sharing of issues. Before I left for Iowa, he suggested to the local mayor that I would be a good candidate for his appointment of a chairman for the first civil rights commission. His reasoning was "Irving can do it."

I met two individuals in a Minneapolis Toastmasters Club—John Olson and Keith Frost. They were excellent for synergy in discussing business issues. We would meet for lunch twice a week. It was a joke among us that they would come with ideas, and at the next session, "Irving would have done it" and be able to tell them what works and what doesn't. About two weeks ago I called Keith from Arizona, and he was dying from cancer. John had died about two years earlier. John and Keith for years had pushed me to write this book. As he signed off he said, "Your book will be done because Irving can do it. Adios my friend." He died the next day.

When I was in Iowa I was so immersed in my work that I felt I needed an outlet where I could relax. Years before I had played sax and clarinet in a professional dance band. For a minimum investment I refurbished the sax I had used in college. I started by playing behind closed doors!

About this same time I was looking for a medical director for the company. I found a doctor in a single practice in a small community that was located five miles from the company. I felt he would meet our needs. His name was Dale Everson. While I was trying to nurture a relationship with him, I found out that Dale was the founder and director of a music show in the area that raised money for charity. To support the show, Dale had organized a small band. The stage would hold a limited number of members and it had become so popular that once you joined the band, you were in it for life. Thus Dale was very careful about whom he invited to join.

One evening he invited my wife and I for dinner along with the band director for the college, his brother-in-law. Before I finished my meal, Dale's wife, who was a no-nonsense get things done person, said, "Let's have some music." I had an alibi since I didn't have my old sax with me. They said they could solve that because the college director had a trunk full of reed instruments. We had fun but I quickly realized I was being auditioned for a seat in the community band!

I got so involved in this new venture that it cost me three new saxophones and a clarinet—an expensive evening! I've always said that a true friend has the capacity to make you better than you are. Dale, through music, did that for me. We played many a gig beyond the show. My favorite memory was a Pete Fountain rendition Dale wrote of "It's been a long, long time" that I did with the chorus.

An uncle of mine, who everyone called Boxy, was another great mentor. Not only did he show confidence in my ability to get things done but he showed me the merit of a good sense of humor, and by example, to never use profanity. We frequently fished together, and one day we decided to beach the boat on shore when we returned to the cabin. He decided to give one last big pull on the oars to get the boat up on the beach as far as possible. However, there was a tree root under water, which you couldn't see. The boat hit the tree root and abruptly stopped. We both fell off our seats, the tackle was strewn all over the bottom of the boat, our glasses were bent and our caps were cockeyed. He looked at me from under his cap and said, "Irv, please say something appropriate!"

What I learned about the strengths or traits that helped me the most in my efforts to be a servant leader:

1. **Visionary**: I think in terms of four simple considerations. a) Listen to input from those you're serving. b) Keep the plan simple. c) Be persuasive in selling the plan. d) Be tenacious in achieving the plan.

Questions to consider if you want to be a servant leader:

1. Identify some friends who could form a life-giving (no one dominates) spiritual support group.

2. What lessons did you learn from a mentor?

Chapter Seven

I NEEDED A COACH

We had made significant and progressive changes to break away from being the parochial company we had been in the past. New products were introduced, changes were made in the organizational structure, new data processing systems were introduced, and changes were implemented in staffing. We even changed our name from Lutheran Mutual, a name adopted in 1938, to Century Life of America to better represent our marketing efforts.

But now we were in the war zone, and the rate of change was moving exponentially. Our staid old company was going to have to increase the rate of change, and I would have to lead the way. There would be a great deal of misunderstanding and suspicion about motives. The bridge of trust that I had worked so hard to build over the past seven years would be stretched to the limit. It would be a lonely job, and I had no one to talk to. I needed to do everything possible to avoid making cumulative mistakes. The company had to go through a total transformation, and I wanted to avoid my own blind spots and prejudices.

I decided I needed a sounding board—someone I could talk to, someone who would listen to my frustrations, challenge my plans, and keep asking searching questions. He or she didn't have to know our business, but they needed to have an extremely high threshold of curiosity and an ability to listen and provide candid feedback. I didn't expect the sounding board to tell me what to do. It had to be my plan. I had to take ownership and responsibility for the future. I couldn't pass the buck, but I had to minimize any miscues.

Hiring a Personal Coach

Hiring a personal coach was obviously helpful in establishing a vision by listening to all sides of an issue and communicating effectively where we were headed as an organization. Not many stones were left unturned.

One of the frequent reasons given for the failure of mergers is the personal agenda or the ego needs of the CEO. If you make an honest personal assessment of your ego needs and conclude that they are very important, a coach is a must. An open and honest psychological contract with a personal coach can mitigate against letting ego get in the way of meeting the needs of the total organization. The relationship with the coach should be very confidential, direct, and honest with no holds barred. As Patrick Lencioni stated in his book *The Five Temptations of a CEO:* "choose trust over invulnerability."

A number of years ago I was chair of the board of regents of a college. It was during the time when there was a high turnover in the CEOs of colleges. It was very obvious that those CEOs who instinctively made it a practice to solicit input from any source they could tap were surviving the traumatic changes that were occurring. We all have personal blind spots we need to avoid when changes are dramatic. A coach can alert one to those spots.

A coach can also help in pushing the CEO to the

point where the vision is clear and the communications of the vision much more crisp. Being alert to how communications will be heard is extremely important. (Two excellent references on coaching to consider are *Executive Coaching* by Mary Beth O'Neill and *Enlightened Leadership* by Ed Oakley and Doug Krug.)

In my search for the right person, I checked with the head of Human Resources for one of our industry organizations for some names to consider. He gave me two names that were at the top of his list—one was an industrial psychologist teaching at a university just 20 miles from our office! He was well-organized, disciplined in his thinking, very curious, and could ask a ton of searching questions. Our relationship developed to the point where we wasted zero time on chit chat and were able to get right to the heart of an issue. We were openly honest and frank with each other, so the synergy was amazing.

I didn't realize it at the time, but there was a new concept gaining popularity in this country called "life coaching." It is defined as a powerful alliance designed to forward and enhance the lifelong process of human learning, effectiveness, and fulfillment. In effect I had hired my own personal coach.

It was the best decision I made in picking up the pace of the transformation I had started.

Our board of directors, while supportive, looked with a jaundiced eye at me when I said I was retaining a personal coach. True, in a sense any member of the board could have filled the role of coach. But what I needed was someone who would be on call 24/7.

Following are three areas in which I found my coach to be particularly helpful.

1. Creating a climate for change

I reviewed with my coach all the changes I had made during the comfort zone period. We discussed ways in which decisions could be made much quicker and with even greater sensitivity to the culture. The number of meetings with managers, associates, the community, and the local newspaper were increased. We named a communications guru to make sure we weren't missing something.

My coach would periodically sit in on some of my meetings, and we would follow them up with not only a performance appraisal of how I did but also discuss what we heard and how it would shape the future.

2. Dealing with individual problems

I called my coach late one night and set up an appointment to meet him for breakfast at 6 AM to discuss a plan I had for dealing with a distribution problem. Agents were telling their companies that they would keep the clients' business with the company if the company would pay some of the high early commissions to the agent. It simply wasn't fair to the client to once again incur those extra expenses. I had to find a way to protect the interests of the policyholders.

A few companies had made changes to cope with what was happening in the economy, which had a negative impact on the agents who distributed the company's products. The situation had become critical as agents began to take the business they had written and move it to another company. In fact in a few cases it became so serious that regulators stepped in to avoid critical impairment of a company's surplus.

I was trying to work with all the interested parties to come up with a solution that would be a win-win one for both the company and the distribution system. We went back and forth on the issue and at 8 AM I held a breakfast meeting (my second for the day) with the associates affected. The meeting went well because I had thought through the various options and was in a position to anticipate their reactions. I was well prepared.

The egg-throwing harassment in the community, mentioned earlier, helped me to realize there were community groups outside the company intensely interested in what we were doing. It was necessary for me to play an active public relations role, especially in a small town where suspicion and distrust could have a negative impact on the associates and their families in ways that could affect morale within the company. This required me to delegate a number of internal responsibilities to others if I was to be the spokesperson to the community. Otherwise I ran the risk of spreading myself too thin. As a result, I shifted some of the work assignments and reduced the number of senior officers reporting to me from six to four.

The option I considered and adopted at one of our periodic brainstorming sessions was to assign one of our bright young men to the role of sweeping up after me (the "sweeper" mentioned earlier) on detail, documentation, and follow up. This young man attended every meeting I attended. He kept a record of decisions made and who was to do what to follow up on decisions.

A special problem arose. We had a long-term associate who was considering organizing an opposition to the course of action the company was taking. In the meeting with my coach I considered two options: 1) letting him go; or 2) keeping him employed by listening to his concerns and getting him involved in the solution. I took the second option. With the blessings of his manager, I used him as a resource for ideas when dealing with his phase of the business. While it meant more travel for me since his office was not within the small community, he became a trusted partner, and his input was constructive. It worked.

One evening I called my coach to discuss with him over the phone a situation where one of the associates was considering bolting from my attempts to affiliate with the other company. He was one of the point individuals in my plans, and I needed him to be involved. A misunderstanding had developed over the organization of one of the functions that was to be consolidated between the two companies.

We discussed the source of the problem and the options I had to resolve it. The next morning I called for the corporate plane, which was on another mission, picked up the associate, took him directly to the source of the problem, and within a matter of hours hammered out an amicable solution. With an effective sounding board, I had the benefit of an objective approach to the resolution of an issue and could deal with it in a deliberate, constructive manner.

My coach was also valuable in helping me address concerns of the board and the strategies used to keep them engaged and constructive. It was in discussions with my coach that I decided there was the need for a special board committee to deal with affiliation issues. As a result the board appointed a three-member ad hoc committee. Members appointed to the committee had experienced dramatic change in their own companies. The committee met between board meetings on an as needed basis and in turn reported to the total board at their quarterly meeting. From the board's perspective, they were more involved in the rapid changes that were taking place, and it gave me another creative resource to work with in the change process. The result was that it strengthened the board/CEO partnership.

3. Monitoring communications

I asked my coach to sit in on some of our senior staff meetings so that together we could improve the process. As a result I started identifying agenda items as either a "1" or "2." A "1" meant that I would identify the issue and then solicit comments. Once I felt that everyone had provided their input, I would make the decision. We simply didn't have time to function by consensus. A "2" meant that I had made a decision, but they had a "need to know" for effective communications throughout the organization.

With input from my coach, I developed a plan for communicating on a regular basis with associates. To avoid misunderstanding where people were reluctant to bring up questions in large groups, we had pre-communications meetings with the managers. The purpose of these meetings was to advise them as to what I would be saying. I also asked them to "Tell me what I said." By listening I could massage my communications to be more effective. Also the managers had an obligation to correct associates if there was a misunderstanding. The procedure helped the effectiveness of communications and minimized rumors.

From the Corporate Notebook

SIT LOOSE

I have a tendency to be too driven, too focused when I have a specific objective. I found it helpful to try to find the humorous side of what we were doing or to make light comments during periods of tension. Frequently some staff member would say to me, "I knew everything was going to be okay because I could hear you laugh." I also tried to set aside times for R and R. My coach regularly checked to see that I kept a balance in my life.

I don't remember the Bible verse but I remember the place, the speaker, and the central message. The message was "We need to learn to sit loose." Some techniques I've used to achieve that objective are:

• Ask myself the question regarding the issue I'm dealing with, "Will it be important five years from now?"

• Look for the humor in what we are doing.

• Be willing to laugh at yourself.

• Consider the possibility of non-offensive practical jokes.

• Get involved in a hobby. In my case that was music.

One humorous incident that began with serious overtones occurred after we had created a lake between the office and the community. One day a staff member came running into my office announcing that the lake was disappearing! Sure enough, as I looked out of the window in horror, I could see our large lake gradually disappearing. The first image that came to mind was a minor tsunami running down Bremer Avenue, the main street in the community.

We notified local authorities about what had happened and found that there was a series of caves in the area, which led to the river further down stream. Evidently our lake had drained down through the cave system into the river. The river had risen somewhat, but thankfully there was no flooding in the town. We made the lake smaller, keeping it away from the caves, and the problem was solved.

Of course this incident was top local news. When I was questioned about it by a reporter after we understood the problem and knew the solution, I simply said in jest, "We decided to drain the lake in the fall and will refill it next spring!"

The importance of not taking life too seriously was driven home to me when I was in Minneapolis, working in a very political environment. As a result, I developed an ulcer. Getting out of that environment into something where I could follow my own personal philosophy and be my authentic self resulted in the ulcer disappearing.

I shared my philosophy of sitting loose with one of the company field managers. He appreciated some things we had done in a year in which he was very successful. He gave me a Mickey Mouse watch to remind me to sit loose. I have now worn that watch for 25 years. The affiliation was long and arduous, but we had fun while doing well.

What I learned about the strengths or traits that helped me the most in my efforts to be a servant leader:

1. **Sit Loose:** Many times during the difficult years I heard the statement, "I knew what we were doing was okay, and we would someday

reach our objective because I could hear you laughing." It's important to try to relax and enjoy the journey.

Question to consider if you want to be a servant leader:

1. In what ways do you sit loose?

2. How can you do it more effectively?

From the Corporate Notebook

INTEGRITY IS THE ISSUE

The following story illustrates how some of the characteristics of my definition of a servant leader have been part of me for a long time. If I had used a coach at the time in my life when I ran away from home, I probably would have found a more negotiable solution.

The first love of my life happened to be Catholic. My parents were adamant that after I had dated her one year as a junior in high school, I should terminate the relationship based on the girl's religion. I decided that their demand was unacceptable. One day when they were gone, I left a note on the kitchen table that told them I was leaving because of their prejudice. I took my bag and hitchhiked to Minneapolis. I found a third story, non-air conditioned apartment and an evening job at the post office sorting mail.

Micah 6:8 has been a guiding principle for me for many years. I've paraphrased that verse and put it on my computer screen, using three words: INTEGRITY – EMPATHY – HUMILITY to represent the core of my authentic self.

What I learned about the strengths or traits that helped me the most in my efforts to be a servant leader:

1. **Integrity**: This strength is so important that you should do everything you can to make it transparent. Again to paraphrase Emerson, "What you do is so important I can't hear what you say." It should be obvious to your staff that you "walk the talk."

Questions to consider if you want to be a servant leader:

1. How would I define my authentic self?

2. What do I need to do to achieve that?

Chapter Eight

RICK WARREN WAS RIGHT, IT'S NOT ABOUT ME

I f one is sincere about sustaining the organization, the first priority should be to develop and build human resources. It is the most important asset of any organization. Two examples of how I tried to nurture this asset follow.

When we started to change the culture of the company, there would inevitably arise misunderstanding among associates. I tried to explain that there are very few people in this world who wake up in the morning with the attitude of "I'll get so and so today." When there is a difference of opinion, assume the other's good intentions. Start to resolve the issue by assuming there is a misunderstanding. Anytime we saw someone consciously do this we would give them an "AGI" (assume good intentions) saying, "Well done!" This practice was particularly helpful when we were consolidating two companies with their different cultures.

I always tried to know not only all associates by their first name but also their spouses. I'll always remember the 100th anniversary convention we held where approximately 600 home office and field associates and their spouses were in attendance. It was quite a challenge. Some associates would try to confuse me by coming up to me with some one else's spouse!

The impartial manner in which future leadership was selected preserved the asset we had worked so hard to nurture. When I retired I was asked if I would consider the traditional role of "consulting." I said, "No, the associates who are in place are very capable of carrying on the mission. I've done everything I can do, don't feel you need to call me. I'll call you."

For several years prior to the affiliation, we

spent significant time and energy in developing our greatest asset, our associates. If we both integrated our human resources and consolidated functions between the two companies, we could be assured that the affiliation would become permanent. It was like scrambling eggs—there was no way it could be unscrambled—and permanency would be accomplished.

Focusing on Performance Appraisals

Through crisp accountability standards for the corporation, the departments, and individuals we became a "tighter" organization—much more creative, proactive, and accountable for results. Developing a "tighter" organization inherently means the company mission evolves with a greater sense of urgency. I've often said that as the organization matured, there was no way I could look at the future of the company through rose colored glasses, and gloss over the trouble spots in the future to convey a better picture. They wouldn't have let me get away with it. The culture of the company had changed.

I wish every business leader would consider the merits of broadening and intensifying their company performance appraisal system. The climate for performance surveys, attitude surveys, department "physicals," reviewing individual performance appraisals with the industrial psychologist, individual development plans, and my visibility in the process paid off in the end. The inventory of human resources indicated that individual development plans uncovered untapped potential. If we hadn't used it through the affiliation process, the company would very likely have lost a very valuable resource.

We integrated functions in the location where there was a natural employment base and used the following process to de-emphasize the politics of assigning associates to a particular job and location:

• Three members from each board of directors were assigned to oversee the process.

• The integrated jobs were profiled ten years into the future.

• Candidates for the integrated jobs were all given up-to-date, psychological assessments.

• The CEO from the two companies, the senior human resources person from each company, the industrial psychologist who did the assessments, and a senior consultant who reported to the joint board committee reviewed each job and prioritized candidates.

- Positions were then assigned according to the employee's ability and capacity to grow into a future role. The process worked in effect like a professional sports draft.

- Once the senior positions were assigned, the process was repeated throughout the organization with the addition of the newly appointed supervisors who would participate in the process for his or her unit.

The associates from the smaller company had an opportunity in the new company. We had spent years in identifying the potential capacity of each individual associate followed by a development plan to meet that objective. The years of work put into developing the organization paid off. Associates were prepared to accept broader responsibilities.

During my 47 years in business, I can count on one hand the number of times that I received an effective performance appraisal. It was usually "You're doing fine. We're increasing your compensation by X dollars!" I believe that's the experience of many, but we had to do much better than that to build a tight organization.

A thorough performance appraisal should last from two to four hours. In addition, I chose to focus on a multi-faceted tighter approach to our performance appraisal process at the corporate level, the department level, and the individual level. I started by monitoring my own performance as a means for demonstrating my commitment to its use as a valuable professional development tool.

We developed an action plan to improve the "climate for performance." Every two years we would redo the study to measure how much progress we had made compared to our previous study and what we should do next to further improve the climate for performance.

In the year in which we were not doing a climate for performance survey, we did the traditional employee attitude survey.

A greater volume of business and a number of different products—for instance, more asset accumulation products than life insurance—meant different expertise and staffing in the future. As we considered what the company would look like ten years into the future, it became clear that some departments would have to make drastic changes. By using an outside resource, we did a "physical" of the department to compare the current profile of the unit to what it would need to look like in ten years. We then developed an action plan to build the unit in order to be more proactive than reactive.

My coach helped us structure meetings within the office to make sure 1) there was an advance agenda, 2) leaders were helped in how to effectively work the agenda, and 3) assignments were made including a follow-through process.

For Individuals

I had psychological assessments completed on all individuals that were managing associates. We also offered the service for others who wanted it. The purpose of these assessments was to help the company manage our most important asset—our human resources. We tried to be more effective in determining where in the future the associate might have the best opportunity to utilize his or her strengths in the company. If strengths were innate but not developed, we followed through with a development plan to reach the associate's objective. Assessments were updated every three years.

Some people are threatened by psychological assessments, and I have been criticized for placing too much emphasis on them. The best I could do was to lead by example and point out that the instrument is just a guide and the final cut is made between the supervisor and the associate.

The assessment is just one of the instruments used in helping to shape the career of an individual. What we were after as a company was to provide a climate that would encourage the associates to stretch so that they could reach their career objectives.

Contextual Performance Appraisals

Periodic performance appraisals are essential but probably the most effective are the ones that immediately follow an incident. These, of course, should include both affirmation and corrective change. The following is an example of how we implemented this strategy.

At one of our senior officer meetings I described an agenda item where I needed input. I asked for opinions from everyone. After the discussion, which was divided about even, I indicated my decision. The associate, who had offered a different opinion, threw his papers down with an attitude which reflected obvious disgust. After the meeting I went to see him in his office and told him what I had observed and asked him what he recalled from the incident. He didn't acknowledge what happened, but it never occurred again.

Performance appraisals typically tend to be generic and not specific. Contextual performance appraisals are specific because the event is timely and fresh in one's mind and much more effective and motivating.

It was important that all employees knew that the new discipline in performance appraisal applied to everyone in the organization, including me. Periodically I had my coach sit in on meetings with my senior officers to make sure they were timely and productive. He didn't participate in the meeting, but afterwards the two of us would meet and critique the session. The purpose was to give me a performance appraisal on the meeting. Associates knew I was having the follow-up meeting and the reasons behind it.

I wrote out performance appraisals for those reporting to me and reviewed them with my coach in advance. Again the staff member knew that this process was a part of my evaluation, and I was demonstrating the importance of performance appraisals throughout the organization.

BUILDING LIFE-GIVING RELATIONSHIPS

In the dedication of this book I gave a definition of a life-giving relationship, which deserves repeating. It came from a friend who spent an evening with us and sent us a poetic note of thanks. That note read in part as follows: "The dance you two do is filled with extravagant loving and delight in living. It's enveloping and encouraging, warm and vital!"

If a relationship is not life-giving, it is narcissistic, boring, and sucks the energy out of you. It has been frequently stated that we're in a generation where it is all about me. In a servant-led organization it is not about ME, or greed, it's about YOU—all of the stakeholders.

To lead a company through a transformation, you need to focus on building life-giving relationships. It means being very open and honest. Know your staff and their concerns. Listen, listen, listen! Let no one dominate the conversation. If necessary, agree to disagree.

I once read a statement in a book about what

the Bible says regarding relationships, which I will never forget. It stated, "To your face I speak with utter frankness but behind your back I speak with the utmost pride." Creating this kind of environment resulted in some memorable experiences.

We tried to do something unique for the staff members who had faithfully served the company for more than 45 years, in addition to the normal service gifts. For example, one diligent associate would bring a banana to work every day to eat at coffee break time. I had the staff write a simulation of an annuity, which would give her a banana a day until her retirement. We made it look very official and had the local grocery store deliver a bunch of bananas every Monday just for her!

I remember one other incident where an employee had spent many months traveling. He was approaching his 45th anniversary with the company. I talked his wife into keeping a secret and then asked him and his wife if they would accompany me to Minneapolis to interview a candidate for the field organization. What he didn't know was there was no candidate. I took him and his wife to a downtown motel in Minneapolis where they stayed for a long weekend. I flew home and left the car with them.

These two stories illustrate that personal expression of appreciation is more important than the "gold watch." Show them that you are aware of their commitment to the organization. Show intense interest in their issues.

When you create a life-giving relationship with a staff member through synergy you: 1) enrich life between the two of you, 2) enrich the life of the organization, and 3) enrich the life of the people you serve. The two words that best express the qualities to focus on are: empathy and humility. The best illustration I can give of an organization that understands what I'm talking about is the Mayo Clinic.

For more than 30 years I have had periodic check ups and occasionally treatment at either the Mayo facility in Rochester, Minnesota, or the one in Scottsdale, Arizona. Hundreds of people go through those facilities every day, and yet in all that time, I have never met any member of the staff that didn't make me feel that I was important and the only individual they had to deal with at the moment. They intently focus on you. That kind of empathy and humility will build life-giving relationships.

What I learned about the strengths or traits that helped me the most in my effort to be a servant leader:

1. **Empathy**: Try to put yourself in the staff members shoes to understand their issues.

2. **Humility**: Listen, listen, listen. In a servant led organization your needs are secondary to the needs of staff.

Questions to consider if you want to be a servant leader:

1. What techniques could you use to build life-giving relationships?

2. How could you encourage open and honest dialogue with your staff?

Chapter Nine

ELEMENTS OF SUCCESS
IN TIMES OF CHANGE

Just five years after the affiliation between CUNA Mutual and Century, it was evident that the results had exceeded our expectations for the most part. In any innovative venture, there are bound to be lessons learned. In this chapter I will summarize for the reader what has been learned from this experience. I have organized these lessons into four major categories: strategic, cultural, communications, transformation, and governance plus further additional issues.

STRATEGIC ISSUES:

- Keep strategy ahead of structure.
- Develop a well-thought-out strategy.
- Develop a plan so that the entire organization will keep a focus on your primary strategy.

CULTURAL ISSUES:

- Understand the difference in corporate cultures and define what type of culture you want to create.
- Develop a method to work through differences in culture.

COMMUNICATION ISSUES:

- Plan and orchestrate communications carefully.
- Do not delay passing on information.
- Do not oversell the change.
- Do not withhold information longer than necessary.
- Do not make promises you cannot keep.
- Be acutely aware of your comments.

TRANSFORMATION ISSUES:

- Appoint a transformation director.
- Senior management should keep hands-on during the change process.
- Clarify the role of any consultant.
- Do not use the most extreme example of your culture as your cultural change agent.
- Have a technique for counterparts in the organizations to become better acquainted.
- Involve human resource staff on the high level transition team.

ADDITIONAL ISSUES:

- The CEO must focus on board integration early in the process.
- Do not depend exclusively on economies of scale to ensure your future.
- Integrate the CEO positions carefully.
- Work hard at keeping your ego under control.
- Strive to create a transparent organization.

GOVERNANCE ISSUES

In a business the CEO is the primary catalyst for setting governance discipline, working collaboratively with the Board of Directors. My objective was to establish a transparent management style in a "Service above self" organization. Governance policies are to be fair and just to all the stakeholders.

The following will describe Governance policies that evolved over several years. The list is not necessarily exhaustive but represents our significant policies.

BOARD OF DIRECTORS
• **Chairperson.** The chair should always be an "outside" stakeholder since he/she should have the primary control of the board agenda. A different member of the board should assume the role of the chairperson every two years to distribute authority among the members.

• **Paid employee.** The only paid employee on the board should be the CEO. Board membership should not be a perk. Staff should attend board meetings as subject matter requires.

• **Board committee membership.** Committee

113

membership should change on a rotating basis every year with staggered terms to provide continuity.

• **Meeting expense.** Since you're setting an example for the rest of the organization no meetings should be held in a resort location unless the members pay the increase expense.

CHIEF EXECUTIVE OFFICER

• **Outside Boards.** Avoid serving on any other board for pay. In particular, avoid "exchanging" board seats with another organization in order to retain objectivity on the board.

• **Charitable organizations.** Commit at least 10% of your time to community and regional charitable organizations. If possible choose commitments that are completed in short periods of time instead of years (for example, fund drives instead of boards).

• **Report to stakeholders.** Make at least annual "state of the company" reports to stakeholders such as community, vendors, retirees, retired directors. Make at least monthly reports to employees.

• **Internal auditor.** Periodically visit with your internal auditor and make sure that if they see something you've done that doesn't look as "clean as a hound's tooth," they owe it to you to tell you immediately.

• **Golden parachutes**. Avoid them! Remember "This is not about me; it's about you." Money can't buy the many thank you notes you'll receive in the following years. They are life giving.

• **Consulting role**. Avoid a consulting role upon retirement. It is an unnecessary perk that is an additional expense to the company and can be confusing to the new management.

• **Compensation**. The current rate of pay for CEOs has been reported to be over 500 times the average rate of pay for employees. This is excessive. For our size of company I favored a multiple of around 10 and part of that in deferred compensation to keep the cost of fringe benefits down.

In the type of culture and corporate governance described we never had a problem recruiting the staff member or board member we were seeking. Except for family emergencies, I don't recall one board member missing a meeting in 17 years. They frequently said that attending a meeting was like attending a "business clinic." They simply didn't want to miss. In addition the staff knew that during the crisis of the transformation all of the changes that were endured were about them and not about me.

Successfully addressing these issues was both a personal and a collective journey of leadership development for me and my associates. While every circumstance and environment is different, there are lessons learned from our journey that can be of practical benefit to others.

Questions to Consider:

1. Are your policies consistent with the above suggestions? If not, what is your justification for the difference?

2. What problems do you see to change your policies?

3. How would you define an acceptable level of compensation? What steps need to be taken to reach the acceptable level?

From the Corporate Notebook

IT REALLY IS A WONDERFUL LIFE!

That line from the movie "It's a Wonderful Life" is almost a cliché, but it speaks to the strong influence we have on the lives of others, usually without our awareness. The direct contact we have is only the beginning. The ripple effect can be enormous!

One day not long ago, I unexpectedly received a packet of letters from a dozen high-ranking staff at the Madison office of CUNA Mutual. It had been more than 10 years since I had worked with any of the writers. I suspect they knew I was writing a book and wanted to share with me the positive impact I had on their careers and their lives. The stories they shared and the apparent ripple impact on their families and other associates were heartwarming. I happened to receive those letters when I needed a lift. What a blessing.

I flashbacked to the daily decisions we faced in transforming the company. During those turbulent times, I kept repeating to myself that the crossroad we were at were "not about me, but about all the other policyholders, associates, community, and vendors." This meant working hard on remembering names, personal stories, concerns, and making sure I greeted everyone by name in social gatherings. It always seemed that my efforts came back many-fold, and in return, I gained strength and conviction.

I wonder if leaders today always realize the long-term impact of today's decisions and their ripple effect. Do they understand the power of their efforts? The letters I received provided insight and inspiration. For George Bailey, the man was shown the impact he had on his community by his guardian angel. After losing the money of the Savings and Loan Association that his uncle owned, the people he had touched rallied around him and gave him the money to meet his need. Every action has consequences—good or bad. Once an action is taken, even if we try to dampen the consequences, that action has consequences we also have to live with. Thus, it is important to do the right thing so that the consequences we live with are good ones.

I often feel like the recipient of the last line of the movie. Remember when Medal of Honor recipient Harry Bailey comes in and toasts his brother, saying "To my big brother George, the richest man in town." I am rich beyond words.

Questions to Consider:

1. How have you had an influence on others? Has it been positive? Has it been negative?

2. What is it you can do to help people? What will make a difference for them?

Chapter Ten

NOW IT'S YOUR TURN

The purpose of writing this book has been primarily to leave a legacy in response to my understanding of the challenge given to all of us in Hebrews 13:7. In the *New International Version* that verse reads as follows:

Remember your leaders, who spoke the word of God to you. Consider the outcome of their way of life and imitate their faith.

To become a servant leader is simply to strive to

become your authentic self, accepting all your shortcomings and benefiting from the mistakes you make during the journey. I've made my share of mistakes, but in the end, the rewards of servant leadership are wonderful.

As I was writing this closing chapter, I received a note from a couple of dear friends in Waverly. The note said, "It must make you feel proud to visit our thriving community. We don't know who said the following, but we think of you: 'We should so live and labor that what comes to us as seed may go to the next generation as fruit.'"

I once heard a paraphrase of the story of Moses who came down from the mountain where he was given the Ten Commandments on tablets of stone. He saw that the Israelites were living a life of greed. He became disgusted and threw the tablets to the ground and broke them.

The next morning he was remorseful and said, "What do I do now, God?" God replied, "There are no other rules to live by. Go back up to the top of the mountain. Life is climbing, not coasting, and start over where you got off the track. That is a blessing not a curse."

Then Moses led the Israelites through 40 years in the wilderness. Moses never gave up, he never asked for anything, nor did he inherit anything, but he hung in there and led his people toward the promised land. It was not always easy, but nothing worthwhile ever is. The promised land for all of us is WINNING WITHOUT GREED.

The previous chapters indicate the strengths or traits that I found to be helpful in my attempt to be a servant leader. There is nothing new in this list. I urge you to make your own list. Your list, like mine, will be impacted by your own willingness to be authentic and open to your own vulnerabilities. A summary of those strengths or traits is as follows:

1. Transparency

2. Integrity

3. Development

4. Team

5. Trust

6. Leadership

7. Visionary

8. Sit loose

9. Empathy

10. Humility

The following is a summary of the process for introducing changes I used that worked for me. Your leadership opportunities may be different, but you can use this as a working prototype.

Within a business group:

1. After the associates that reported to me read the material, I held a retreat to solicit ideas on how the information should shape our companies strategy.

2. I reported our plans to our board.

3. I used my coach to monitor progress.

4. I discussed and reported results with all company associates monthly and with our board quarterly.

Within a church council or a community service club board:

1. I held a retreat and had the board discuss in what ways we might, as a group, use the material to function better.

2. I used my coach to monitor progress regularly.

3. Periodically I would review the progress we were making toward our objective.

4. Since this was a part of my education in leadership, I kept notes on what I learned.

There is a statement that can be found in the scriptures that goes something like this: "You will find yourself by losing yourself in service to others." The simple answer to the success story I've shared and the ultimate result of beating the merger odds is servant leadership. If you embark on the journey using the process I've described, remarkable results can be obtained. I urge you to try it. It can be very rewarding.

GOD'S BLESSINGS ON YOU!

QUESTIONS FOR DISCUSSION

On Values:

1. What were some of the basic values informing the strategic planning process described in the book? What role did these values play in the process? Give examples.

2. How do these values relate to the teaching of the Prophets? Of Jesus? Give some examples.

3. What role do you think these values play in the planning and policy decisions of major multinational corporations? What role do you think they could or should play? Do you think it is realistic to expect that the business decisions of major corporations will take these values into serious consideration? Why or why not? What are some of the factors that may have made it less difficult for a company like Century Life of America to practice these values than a company like GE or GM? How could these difficulties be overcome?

4. Do you think these values are applicable in the political sector? Could or should they guide deci-

sions about public policy? Why or why not? To what extent do you think they do inform public policy decisions?

5. What do you think the author understands to be the purpose of business?

NOTES

On Leadership

1. The author speaks about servant leadership. What are some of the characteristics of servant leadership? How does this understanding of leadership compare with Jesus' understanding and practice of leadership? Give examples from Jesus' life and teaching.

2. Give some examples of ways in which the author practiced this form of leadership.

3. How did this way of understanding and exercising leadership contribute to the success of the process?

NOTES

On Method

1. What were the goals of this process? How realistic were they?

2. From the perspective of values, this process was very "idealistic." How did the author balance this idealism with realism? Give examples.

3. How important was analysis in this process? What adjectives would you use to describe the analytical part of the process?

4. How important do you think analysis was in the ministry of Jesus? Give examples to support your position.

5. Changing the culture of an organization or community is one of the most difficult challenges confronting leadership. The response often is, "We have always done it that way." It is surprising that, although this process challenged long-standing company culture and practice and the reorganization of the company resulted in the elimination of some positions, there was minimal internal dysfunction. What are some of the factors that help explain that?

6. What can we learn from this book that might be applicable in our families? In our congregations? In our work place? In our social institutions? How can we begin to apply what we've learned?

NOTES

AFTERWORD

There is extensive material written regarding the impact that different cultures have on a merger. It does not have to be a negative experience. I believe that through the joint effort of the two companies we were able to build a blended culture. Years of building a tight team in the smaller company meant that it could be a contributor to the blended culture and in effect the sum of the two ended up better than either one alone.

The affiliation journey was long and arduous. But nothing really worthwhile is ever easy. The blood, sweat and tears are now past history but there are two stories that I will never forget.

By design the board of directors was a tough minded but fair group of individuals. They were not a "rubber stamp" group. They represented the policyholders and took their responsibilities seriously. I was being innovative, and they, of course, were concerned. As my thinking evolved on the unique approach to consolidating two companies, I became more articulate as to the course of action we should take. When I laid my plans out, one of the more vocal board members asked to meet me later and in some very colorful language said, "I never dreamed this was what you had in mind!" Several years afterwards, he said, "There are two moments in history that I'll never forget: When Neil Armstrong stepped on the moon and when we consolidated these two companies. I never thought it would happen."

The second story is about the associates. They had concerns of course, but they "hung in there" and made it happen. On December 8, 1989 I received a touching letter signed by all 300 associates, which I put in a glass stand so I can read all the signatures on both sides of the letter. Following is that letter in its entirety:

Dear Irv,

1989 has been an exciting and historic year for the company. It has been a year when a new direction has been set for our company, and this new direction holds the promise of continued success for many, many years in the future.

These accomplishments have not come without struggle, pain, and intense effort. No one in our organization has felt this more directly than you personally. The long hours, the continuous travel, and your split home between two locations have not made life easy for you.

You came into the insurance industry when it was a relatively calm, stable, predictable business. Now, in the later years of your career, it has become difficult and chaotic. Many of your peers in other companies have apparently decided to wait out the storm until their retirement, leaving the problem solving to those left behind. You have not. Even though you have earned the right to relax and enjoy your accomplishments, you knew that the company needs more than that if it is to survive.

We thank you for your tireless visionary leadership. Today all of our associates will receive their Productivity Sharing bonuses. It would be nice if we could present you a bonus check equal to the value of your efforts, but no company could afford that. Instead, we give you our thanks, and our pledge of support to make your dreams a reality.

Thanks for a good year.
All of the Company Associates

Through misty eyes I've reread that letter many times. That letter alone made all of the hard work, difficult decisions, personal growth, and perspiration worth it. Making a difference in the lives of those people and generations to come was what it was all about.

ABOUT THE AUTHOR

Irving Burling is a Fellow of the Society of Actuaries. Since retiring as president and chief operating officer of Century Companies of America, he has coached senior executives facing a transformation in their own companies. In addition, he has coached individuals regarding career changes. His previous book was *Achieving Organizational Transformation* (Quorum Books 1996).

To contact the author, e-mail him at the following address: irv@sio.midco.net.